PRAISE FOR YOUR NEXT CHAPTER

'Angela is such a beautiful and brilliant writer. I love her tone, irreverence, deep honesty and compassion. I felt like she was sitting right beside me sharing her heart and soul, urging me to share mine, too. Women need this book. For too long we've not been true to ourselves or our calling. We've been struggling under the weight of the roles we've been conditioned to believe we're destined for: wife, mother, worker, housekeeper ... the list goes on.

We all have something greater inside us, and if it remains unearthed we will never fix the problems our world is facing. If every woman on the precipice of a new chapter in life had this book, imagine the world we could live in. Just imagine.'

—Carolyn Tate, educator and consultant, author of *The Purpose Project* and *Conscious Marketing*, founder of The Purpose Project course

'There's something very special about discovering a book that speaks straight to your heart. It tells you that its author is a kindred soul, a fellow traveller who has ridden the waves of life's lessons with honesty and grace, and tapped into a deeper, innate wisdom that calls out to be shared. *Your Next Chapter* is a must-read for anyone who dares to live the life they know they are truly capable of living.'

—Louise Laffey, creator of The Wish

'As a child of the seventies, I was taught that girls had it all. In a new and liberated world, we could do anything, be anyone we wanted. Fly to the moon? Sure. Become a millionaire? Absolutely. Be the world's best wife, lover, mother, daughter and friend? Well, of course. The only problem was, no one actually told us how we were supposed to achieve all of these things at once.

In this book, Angela has created a framework that both inspires and equips women so that the remarkable future they envision for themselves is finally within reach. With clarity and compassion, she sensitively shares the way forward for women whose personal and professional lives may already have taken many turns.

Your Next Chapter is an inspiring read that will transform the way you think and feel about your life, family and business, and the legacy you would like to leave in our world. Full of practical strategies, real-life stories of achievement, and tools to make your decision-making simpler, *Your Next Chapter* will show you how it really is possible for women to not only dream big, but also to create a fulfilling life and business that is balanced, positive and purposeful.'

—Sonja Walker, founder of Kids First Children's Services

'This is a brilliantly practical and inspiring guide to stepping into your next chapter in life. Angela is the down-to-earth friend you want by your side as you embark on the adventure. I loved it!'

—Susannah Conway, author of *This I Know: Notes on Unraveling the Heart*

'This brilliant book lays out a clear path to confidently move through the discontent and doubt that's holding you hostage and into the purpose that's calling you. It's an affirming blend of practical wisdom and inspirational guidance that will empower you to release your remarkable ideas into the world and live your greatness. Read it today!'

—Barbara Huson, wealth coach and financial therapist, author of *Overcoming Underearning* and *Sacred Success*

'Angela's book comes straight from her heart and speaks directly to mine. Based on her own life events and chapters, and bolstered by her many client experiences and journeys, this book bursts at the seams with authentic, relatable stories, insights, and a range of practical models and steps to suit everyone.

For anyone seeking an actionable roadmap that will enable them to dream about, explore, develop and/or take action on their next chapter —whether it's the first, fifth or fifteenth—this book provides the way. It is peppered with feeling, passion and commitment. I've known Angela for years, and she continues to surprise, delight and inspire me as she dances along her own "growth edges".'

—Jo Hanlon, leadership, mindset and HR coach

'In these changing times, it's easy to fall into self-doubt and inertia. *Your Next Chapter* is the perfect antidote to help you get unstuck, take action and gain control, to create an extraordinary business.'

—Jane Anderson, Thought Leadership Marketing

'Angela has the gift of clarity and leadership. She takes you by the hand, sharing stories and insights that lead you to your own realisations, and there is nothing more powerful. The practical examples, ideas and questions she leaves you with in each chapter make sure that this is not just another book that you enjoy but don't apply. It's like having your own personal coach in your back pocket. To read this book and do the work is to be transformed, inspired by your own abilities and determination, knowing that you *do* have the resources and resilience to create anything your heart truly desires.

This a no-fluff value-packed gift for all women, but especially those who are ready to change their lives. I know I will come back to this book again and again, not only for its ideas and inspiration, but just to hang out a bit with Angela.'

　—Donna Brown, global business strategist

'If only I had the confidence, I'd start my own business. How many of us have said those words to ourselves? Angela Raspass has done a fabulous job of providing a road map—both practical and philosophical—to help you move forward and create the success, abundance and happiness you deserve. So, if you're tired of staying stuck in inaction, read this book. The world needs your contribution now more than ever.'

　—Lynn A Robinson, author of *Put Your Intuition to Work* and *Divine Intuition*

'I've been waiting for Angela to weave her magic into a book for years, and it's been worth the wait. It's like holding a giant thought-provoking conversation in your hands. You can hear her guiding you with each word. This is an extraordinary tool to inspire change and help you create your amazing next chapter.'

—Samantha Leith, speaker and coach

'After being a part of Angela's world for several years and working intimately with her, I have come to understand and appreciate the gift of a next chapter. We women often place ourselves at the end of the queue, dismissing the cravings and gentle whispers that tell us there's something beyond our current reality waiting for us. When you read this book, whether you're seeking to be an entrepreneur or wanting to pursue a passion project, you will feel immense relief in realising you're not alone in yearning for something more, for wanting to step into your full potential.

Angela has a real gift for taking a framework or model and bringing it to life through the stories and pearls of wisdom that are woven into these pages. You will soon see a crystal-clear vision of what is possible for you in your own next chapter.'

—Sarah Tovey, founder of Bloom with Sarah

'Angela has a knack for reaching into an inner world many of us know intimately but haven't articulated. She paints a description of discontent so acutely relatable it's like she's inside our heads, and then gives us a roadmap towards an enchanting new future.'

—Emma Grey, co-author of *I Don't Have Time*, co-founder of My 15 Minutes: Fast Forward Coaching

Ditch your doubt

YOUR

own your worth

NEXT

and build the business

CHAPTER

you *really* want

ANGELA RASPASS

Published 2020 by The Self-Worth Institute Pty Ltd, Sydney, Australia

Copyright © Angela Raspass 2020

www.angelaraspass.com

Title: *Your Next Chapter – Ditch your doubt, own your worth and build the business you really want*

Author: Angela Raspass

Diagrams and models: © Angela Raspass

ISBN: 9780645008104

A catalogue record for this book is available from the National Library of Australia.

Categories: Business | Self-help | Personal development

Book production: www.smartwomenpublish.com

To Graham, who has always encouraged and supported me through every one of my chapters. Thank you for being my original and strongest belief buddy.

CONTENTS

FOREWORD

If this book has made its way into your hands, it's no accident.

Its pages hold a wealth of wisdom and practical advice to help you navigate toward whatever makes you feel more alive, and away from whatever's been weighing you down or just leaving you feeling ho-hum in some aspect of your life.

A quick scan through these pages will show you what it showed me, that Angela has penned an uplifting yet comprehensive and practical manual for all women, everywhere, who find themselves yearning for something more, something different, but are unsure exactly what it is or how to begin.

In my own work emboldening people to live and lead more bravely, I meet many women who feel this way. Clever women, capable women, accomplished and amazing women, yet women who doubt themselves too much and feel as though they are settling for less than the life they want to be living.

Perhaps you are one of them. If so, you're in the right place and you're in the best hands.

I don't say that lightly. Working in the same broad arena as Angela, I meet many coaches, so-called gurus and empowerment experts. Some stand apart from the rest, those rare birds (and blokes) who are continually doing the deep inner work to show up in the world fully connected to their own power—without the fear-driven need to prove, please, preen or protect; people who are committed to using their unique mix of talents and trials for the highest good of humanity. Angela is one of them.

The beauty of a book written by such a beautiful 'human becoming' (let's face it, few of us ever fully arrive) is that it will help you uncover your own calling, and turn your own talents and trials toward a future vision that will light you up and lift you higher.

As someone who feels deeply called to embolden people to rise above the primal fears that hold them hostage, I must warn you that you will need to do just that as you turn the pages that follow.

In fact, that may well be your most critical work of all. To cease all your busy doing (I know you're very good at that; we women generally are) and to become fully present and acknowledge that your fear of being exposed as inadequate or unworthy in some way is driving you to sell yourself short, talk yourself down, and settle for less than the biggest, bravest and most soul-satisfying life you have within you to live. That is, to bring out of the shadows, where it has been occupying the driver's seat in your life, your fear of not being good enough, smart enough, experienced enough, connected enough, young enough, worthy enough or fill-in-the-blank enough.

We all have such fears. They show up in a myriad of ways: as excuses, perfectionism, superiority, self-doubt, addiction, or the highly curated social masks we wear. It is the work of a lifetime to shine a light in the dark places where they live and step fully into the brilliance of the woman we all have within us to become.

This book will help you do just that, by helping you reframe your past through a broader lens, mining its 'gold' and rewriting the story about those experiences that you've allowed for too long to stifle your future. It will then guide you to reconnect to the power within you, to your unique brand of brilliance, your special 'value' proposition in the world, and your ability to make permanent change in those aspects of your life in which you've been too long disempowering yourself.

Finally, it will guide you to paint the highest vision for your future and create a game plan to step through your fears and into action.

That's pretty powerful stuff.

Yet it's all imminently doable. As long as you're ready to do your part.

Are you ready? I hope so.

Will it be easy? Of course not.

All change, even change for the better, is never easy. That's why so many people tiptoe over-cautiously, too comfortably through life, only to make it safely to their death with their songs still in them. It's why too few wake up each morning inspired by the day ahead.

Ironically, as I write this now, I'm looking toward to a new season in my own life. My four children have now all spread their wings, giving me the freedom to spread my own in new ways I've yet to get clarity on. As I sit in curiosity and wonder about what lies ahead, I know for sure that it will require me to practise courage yet again.

Such is life. Everything we yearn for most—and I mean *everything*—requires courage in some form. Likewise, the richly rewarding future you long to create for yourself will require you to embrace discomfort and put your vulnerability on the line in some way. Just as mine will.

So, keep your pen handy as you read through these pages. Be ready to underline those pearls that jump from the page into your heart, to reimagine your future, and to begin mapping out a new path forward.

Your future is unwritten. You are its author. Dare to write a story that, at your life's end, you'll be proud to read and to pass down. Most of all, dare to trust that if something is tugging on your heart you have everything it takes to bring it into reality.

Live bravely, my fellow journeyer. To quote Ram Dass, 'We are all just walking each other home.' This book will guide your heroine's journey back home to yourself and toward the future you were born to live.

Embrace your future for the daring adventure it is.

Your next chapter? You've got this!

Margie Warrell
Leadership facilitator and speaker
Bestselling author of You've Got This; Make Your Mark; *and* Brave

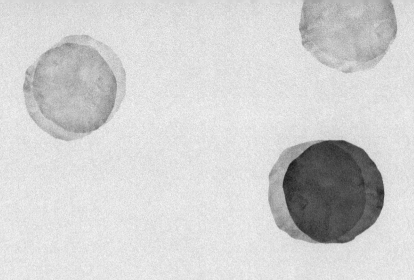

'Life is not just about being inspired. It's about how you inspire others to see themselves.'

Angela Raspass

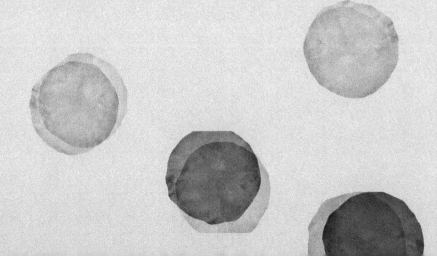

AN INVITATION

Sitting in the meeting, distracted by my mind playing tag with itself as it considered my to-do list, I was really only half listening to the speaker. But then she shared an insight that stopped me in my tracks and seared itself into my heart: 'There's a Susan-shaped hole in the universe, and my job, my only job, is to fill that hole.'

The speaker was talking about her sense of purpose and meaning in the world. The unique calling that only she could hear, that only she could respond to. The persistent calling that asked her to expand right out to her edges. Hearing her describe it in this way was one of those pivotal moments when I recognised a universal truth. This simple wisdom has guided me ever since, and now I'd like to pass it on to you in these pages.

Lovely reader, perhaps you've picked up this book because your own hole in the universe is calling to you and it's becoming difficult to ignore. Perhaps we share the view that life's too short not to be doing the work in the world you are here for.

If that's how you feel, you're in good company.

Although certainty is seldom available in today's unpredictable world, many of us are fortunate enough to be living in a society where our physiological and safety needs are met. When we have this luxury, we also have the space and opportunity to contemplate purpose.

I've found that we tend to move towards our purpose in chapters. Change happens gradually. You make incremental adjustments in your personal landscape, moving ever closer to a sweet spot of contribution and fulfilment that lights you up. And you stay there, sometimes for years until, inevitably (because we are all here to grow), you notice a gentle but insistent pull of discontent and feel drawn towards change again.

You're following an internal compass that no one else has access to, and you need to trust your intuition, take your own counsel and learn as you move, course-correcting through experience and growing insight.

But change can also be thrust upon you in ways you could never have predicted. Separation, divorce, redundancy, bankruptcy, and the death of a loved one are just some of the situations that can be sudden, harsh and gut-wrenching, often leaving you feeling powerless and shell-shocked. When you're in the midst of major upheaval, it's almost impossible to see the value in the experience. Next chapters are often built on skinned knees, but it's not until you look back from the other side of the canyon that you can quietly marvel at your resilience, ingenuity and strength. That's when you may realise that you now have immensely valuable understanding to share that will help others who are still in the fire.

The truth is, a next chapter can arrive at any age, at any time. Some are planned and some are unexpected. Some are significant game changers, where others are mere footnotes in the story of our busy lives.

My first was when I left New Zealand in 1988 on my nineteenth birthday, coming to Sydney for what I planned to be a three-month adventure.

My next was at the age of thirty-four, when, with a baby, a toddler and two bonus boys, my husband's sons from his first marriage, I realised that returning to corporate-land was not for me, and I started my first business, eager for flexibility and income.

Three years later, a major new chapter emerged when I finally escaped a serious addiction that had dogged me for years.

Yet another began when I chose to close my marketing agency and shifted from consulting to mentoring. Without a doubt, there are more chapters waiting for me, and I now know to welcome every one of them.

WHY IS THIS BOOK IMPORTANT FOR YOU?

Danish writer Søren Kierkegaard said, 'Life can only be understood backwards, but it must be lived forwards.' When I turned fifty in 2019, I began to take stock of where I had been and where I was going. I contemplated the words I had heard from so many of my clients and friends: 'If only we'd known what we know now ten, fifteen, twenty years ago.' I blended this observation with a key point from the brilliant book by Australian author Bronnie Ware, *Top 5 Regrets of the Dying*: 'I wish I'd had the courage to live a life true to myself, not the life others expected of me.' When I did this, three things became clear to me:

1. I wanted to encourage more women to consciously choose their next chapters rather than allowing them to simply happen.
2. I didn't want any women to stay where they were if they were not happy—in a job, a business or any other scenario—for a second longer than they had to.

3.   I wanted to ensure that more women recognised the value of their unique experience and how they can harness, shape and share it to help others, if they choose to.

This book offers a roadmap for you to navigate your own journey, regardless of your stage of life. I encourage you to dive in and pull out the messages, practices, tools and ideas that resonate with you so you can move through your next-chapter change cycle with awareness.

And now to my fellow midlifers ...

YOU ARE IN THE MIDST OF A REVOLUTION

The modern workforce and business landscape have changed enormously since we entered them some twenty to thirty-five years ago. This landscape is now fractured, segmented and expanded. In many ways it has been completely remade, its very core and definition revamped. And thus, both the timeline and trajectory of our working lives have been reset.

At midlife, my mother wasn't considering career reinvention, and she certainly wasn't thinking about how she might channel her life experience into a business that would sustain her through her fifties, sixties and beyond. The expectations society had for her, and the opportunities available to her, were considerably different and definitely more limited than they are for women today.

I grew up in a small country town in New Zealand, and during the mid-eighties the Girls Can Do Anything national campaign rang in my ears as I began to search for my own place in the world. There were few examples around me of female business owners. Entrepreneurship, at that stage, wasn't widely discussed in my home or community, and so it did not enter my mind as a possibility when I began to create my own life plan.

How things have changed since then.

In 1999, thirty-one percent of business owner/managers in my adopted home of Australia were women; in 2019 that number had risen to just less than thirty-five percent.[1] The change hasn't been fast, but it has been sustained over a period of time and appears to be continuing.

As midlife women, we are at the forefront of this phenomenon, with the median age of female business owners being forty-seven, slightly younger than the median age of forty-eight for men. I find this hugely exciting.

If you have children, by this stage of your life they're probably becoming more self-sufficient. Some, like my own son, may even have left home. The empty-nest syndrome is not quite as abrupt today as it was in the past because most women have worked in some capacity during their lives. Even so, when the more hands-on parenting responsibilities recede, your own values and desires can be brought into focus again.

The next chapter of your life is opening wide, and you now have enormous life and business wisdom and experience to share in a different way, or at a different level. You may be drawn to entrepreneurship for the first time, or perhaps you have an existing business you want to revitalise, realign, expand or let go of so you can move in the direction that's calling you now.

A SENSE OF PURPOSE IS YOUR ANCHOR

One of the most valuable ways you can channel your experience is through the lens of a business. It allows you to manifest your sense of purpose in tangible ways as you make a difference in the lives of others.

Brené Brown, one of my mentors, says it so well: 'Midlife is when the universe gently places her hands upon your shoulders, pulls you close, and whispers in your ear: *I'm not screwing around anymore. Use the gifts you were given.*'

When you are anchored in a personal sense of meaning—to a cause, community or calling—your contribution has the capacity to fulfil you deeply. There's another significant benefit on offer, too: you will age better physically, mentally, emotionally and spiritually, and this is not just theoretical or wishful thinking on my part. The School of Medicine at the UC San Diego Center for Healthy Aging conducted many studies indicating that having a clear purpose in life is associated with better physical and mental wellbeing as we age.[2]

When you consciously choose to step into your next chapter with focus and anticipation, ready to be challenged and stretched, equipped with the tools that can help you expand and create a ripple of positive impact, your life will become very full. Your spirits will soar. Any feeling of flatness you might think of as frivolous or ungrateful (look at my life, how can I complain?) but may nevertheless have been lurking in the corner of your heart will recede, replaced by what I call 'joy jolts': delicious, sudden infusions of intensely positive emotions that will fill your body, mind and soul right to its edges.

I want more of those joy jolts. And I want them for you, too.

You don't need to fall prey to any outdated, completely irrelevant 'midlife crisis' narrative. Like many of my peers, I choose to challenge and replace that notion with a clear understanding of the power of the midlife expansion.

In *Your Next Chapter*, I show you how to develop your vision, and gain the confidence to design and deliver your ideas and experience to the world, your way. This book is designed to walk you through the steps in the simple Your Next Chapter change cycle. I developed this model after looking back and making sense of my own journey, and then working with many other women and clients who were negotiating the same challenges and stages. Now you can begin to explore what's possible for you, too, as you expand fully into the woman you are becoming.

The model has two phases: 1) *deliberation*, which encompasses the experiences of discontent and desire, and 2) *doing*, which comprises design and delivery. In each phase you'll acknowledge the interference caused by self-doubt, fear, misbeliefs and uncertainty that can create difficulties, detours and even temporary derailments. The two phases are intersected by a decision.

This book covers each step in the change cycle, explaining how it tends to manifest and how to work through it. As your own fresh story unfolds and you become familiar with each stage and its specific stumbling blocks, characteristics and potential, you'll have a guide to move through with greater ease as you create your own next chapter.

I highly recommend you keep a journal with you as you read *Your Next Chapter*. I'm sure you'll be inspired and challenged to capture and expand your existing ideas.

In addition, I have put together a selection of handy resources that will support you in bringing the ideas in this book to life. This includes free access to my online program, Your Journey Board, which will help you to develop and connect to your purpose and vision statement. I take you through this process with audio guides and downloadable PDF workbooks across three modules:

Module One: Finding the Gold in Your Past
Module Two: Connecting to Your Present Power
Module Three: Developing a Clear Vision for Your Next Chapter

You can access this and other materials through my website: angelaraspass. com/bookbonuses

And now I invite you to listen to those whispers that have been calling to you and step forward with a fiercely beating heart, inspired by your desire to make a difference.

I can't wait to see what unfolds in your next chapter.

Angela Raspass
Business and life mentor
Founder of The Self-Worth Institute

PART ONE

DANCING
WITH
DELIBERATION

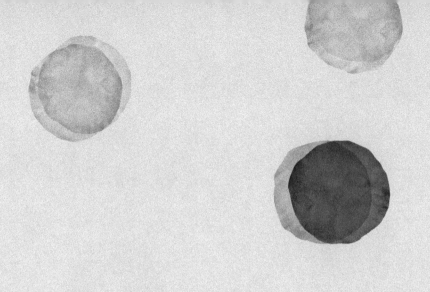

'A woman's discontent increases in exact proportion to her development.'

Elizabeth Cady Stanton

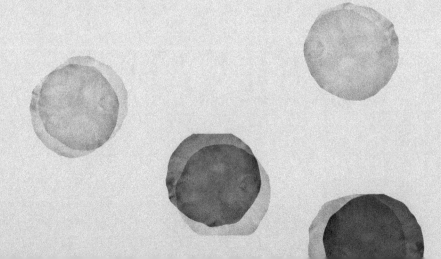

CHAPTER 1

DISCONTENT
A Signpost for Change

As a teenager, I spent many an hour locked away in my room, pouring my heart into my journal. Duran Duran, Culture Club and Spandau Ballet kept me company as I wrote about my hopes and dreams. I was certain I was on the planet for a significant, momentous reason that would be revealed to me when the time was right, quite possibly on a stone tablet, and most likely accompanied by a cacophony of trumpets and the parting of clouds.

In some ways, I feel like I'm still waiting.

I know that this life of mine, when viewed from above some forty years later, has been peppered with wonderful experiences that I'm truly grateful for. I'm not dismissing it or invalidating myself. I can see I've made a difference to a great many people with the work I do, and I often feel grounded and fulfilled. But at the same time I'm aware of experiencing the 'disease of more', an inkling that I've not yet lived up to my potential, that there is more waiting for me, something more to do and contribute to.

That sense of something missing is one I find hard to articulate. I might not expect the stone-tablet delivery anymore, but I still have a hunger inside. It hasn't gone away; it's just been napping. But now it's stretching and unfurling, awake once again, and it wants my attention. It asks me to be all I can be, and sometimes the yardstick it holds up for me can feel a smidgen daunting.

When I've asked other women about this experience, they've been quick to concur that yes, that feeling of discontent and a desire to reach some undefined rung of potential is a familiar one that has nipped at their heels as well, regardless of their achievements.

> *Pascale:* 'Do I think I have unearthed or unrecognised potential? Oh my goodness, yes, absolutely. My current situation comes from having my youngest in her final year of school, and I'm now thinking about what's next as my children become more and more independent and will soon be adults. I gave up a lot in my career to care for my kids. It's not that I regret the time I had with them, but it did mean a different path for my career. Now I wonder what I want to do for the remainder of my working life.'

> *Sally:* 'On one level I'm happy going from day to day, managing to juggle teenage kids, a husband of twenty-seven years, a full-on workload for my business, the washing, cooking and housework, and spending time with friends and extended family.

I can stay in this zone from day to day, week to week, and feel content knowing I'm doing the best I can and that things are okay. But every now and again, usually prompted by a book, article or conversation, a feeling of discontent rises to the surface. Then the questions start: *Time is ticking by, is this all there is? What should or could I be doing before it's too late?*

That unsettles me, makes me feel guilty for not appreciating what I have, and stresses me out for feeling like I have to do more, be more, etcetera, which adds even more pressure. This has been going on for years, but as my kids are getting older, I feel there's something extra now that I haven't been able to define.'

Donna: 'I definitely feel like I've only touched the tip of what I can offer, and this can cause a certain level of anguish.'

Sometimes this experience of feeling that there's something missing generates a push forward, or a burst of enlightenment, and what's missing comes quickly into focus.

Tracy: 'This question of living up to my potential resonates strongly with me. For years I never felt content with what I was doing, earning, or contributing, and whatever I did never seemed enough, or perhaps not quite right. Then the lightbulb moment happened, and I realised my work life was not aligned with my personal values. Since then I've consciously sought to move the two together, and although it's still a work in progress the discontent is lessening.'

Kylie: 'In my middle years I was frustrated at having potential but no time or energy to realise it. Motherhood and a workaholic partner left me carrying the family load. My discontent was a real concern; I worried about when it would be my time. Sometimes it showed up as ego as I fought against feeling invisible and lagging behind my peers.

At times I sought acknowledgement that I'd done a good job. Other times I found myself over-explaining or apologising for not having advanced my career. Luckily for me, I stepped into uncertainty. When I got stuck with a bad boss, I started my own business and now I'm redefining success for me.'

When you view discontent as an invitation to explore something new, its purpose is positive. Discontent can be useful in getting you moving when it's grounded in curiosity and possibility, providing you with energy and enthusiasm to seek growth and new ideas. Discontent has been the launching pad for some significant changes in my own business and life, fuelling me with inspiration and motivation.

But discontent can also have a darker side. If a sense of discontent is generated through watching other people's lives on social media and through other unfair surface-level comparisons, a general sense of not being enough, disappointment and even resentment can appear. When this happens, inspiration and action are seldom side effects.

Sarah: 'Social media can be dreadful for comparison when I'm not feeling on top of everything. I worry that it's too late to have a real impact, especially when I see younger women seemingly killing it on social media. I know logically that it isn't too late, but on my worst days I feel like I've wasted years of my life. I know that's not really true because it's brought a lot of empathy and learning, but I can slip into negativity.

I have big goals and big plans, and most of the time I'm optimistic. But the vulnerability still lies underneath, lurking.'

The keys that allow you to dance with discontent are discernment and critical awareness. When you notice a feeling of discontent, pause and utilise these thought tools. Ask yourself, does the feeling spring from a need to expand, to step up and pursue alignment? Or is it triggered by what you've been told about how success is supposed to look, making you feel you haven't ticked the right boxes? The former is a positive trigger, and it invites growth. The latter comes from a sense of inadequacy that is tied to social conditioning and can take you on an ill-advised detour.

I want you to look back over your life with curiosity and appreciation, recognising the richness of many of the chapters you've already written, the quite amazing things you've done. Take notice of the resilience, flexibility, ingenuity and strengths you've developed as your focus has shifted so many times over the years, by necessity or design.

Different life stages bring new demands, and like most women you have probably managed to respond and juggle various responsibilities deftly, even more so if marriage and motherhood have been a part of your story.

As women, we often experience strong sociological expectations and influences, and pressure to postpone our own desires. As a result, we can put our own needs last, or simply compromise in ways that become habitual over time. Perhaps you have also had the volume turned down on your vision while you've been focused on others, and now you feel that overdue opportunities are available to you.

I'm not suggesting that all women born in the mid-sixties to late seventies, commonly known as Generation X, have been completely subjugated and lack the fortitude to forge their own paths, completely beholden to societal pressure and expectations. They've simply had a lot on their plates, and more was added when they heard that they could 'have it all'. Those women who have managed to stay connected to their innate worth throughout these demanding years of their lives can now bob back up to the surface, ready to respond more fully to their own desires.

Columnist Helaine Olen painted a bleak picture in an article in *The Washington Post*,[3] lamenting that many Generation X women have internalised expectations of effortless self-driven success. In middle age this can lead to self-blame and recriminations if women feel they haven't achieved at the level they think they should have. It's this emotional quicksand that we all need to watch for and be able to navigate our way through.

WHERE DO WE TAKE OUR INSPIRATION FROM?

Every generation of women creates a new path, forged from the progress of those who came before. It seems to me that something changes when we reach this midlife stage of our lives. Our focus broadens and our awareness sharpens. Something asks to be seen. Something unlocks. It's up to us to choose whether or not to respond, to step through the newly opened door and design our next chapter.

You can lift yourself up the priority totem pole, putting you and your needs equal first now as you discover and explore new options. You can connect or reconnect to what's most important to you, and determine the contribution you want to make in the next chapter of your life, in a way that fulfils your desires and aligns with your values. In so doing, you will be able to celebrate and savour the sharp decrease in your concern about what other people think of you and what you do. Put simply, as you mature you will feel less need for approval.

For some women, this self-determination is at the heart of who they are, and consequently they have created lives of great impact and adventure. I asked the members of my own community whom they find inspiring and they were quick to nominate a great variety of women.

Lorraine: 'Jacinda Arden, the prime minister of New Zealand, because she has walked her own path, made hard decisions, and her openness and genuine concern for her fellow humans is heart-warming.'

Deb: 'I'm inspired by Brené Brown's life-changing books, which are an inspiration for anyone wanting to show up in the arena and approach life with courage, embrace vulnerability, and live wholeheartedly.'

Patricia: 'Pema Chodron, an American by birth and a Buddhist nun, takes concepts and helps those of us with Western eyes and minds better understand. She's just so inspiring, and mind- and eye-opening.'

Kirana: 'For me, Suzie Quatro, because she followed her dream. She followed the music she had in herself and listened to it. She created what she needed to create and gave it a unique voice, her *own* voice.'

Pascale: 'Michele Obama is a definite inspiration because of her grace and dignity in the role as first lady, and the values she espouses.'

Rachel: 'Ashton Applewhite, the founder of This Chair Rocks, because she became aware of her own ageism and saw it for what it was, and has made it her life's work to end it for the world.'

Women like these fill us with awe. They are 'way-showers': women who show the way to what's possible. They help us expand our understanding of what can be truly possible, encouraging us to dream a little bigger, aim a little higher. But I also have to admit that for me, these impressive women can be a little far removed from my own life experience. Their accomplishments can feel aspirational, but not necessarily achievable, and women need to feel that their goals are achievable for them to take consistent, confident action.

My thoughts recently strayed to a friend who has welcomed foster children into her home for several years, showing them what love and security look and feel like. Lisa saw gaps in the system and decided to take action. As I write, she is working on establishing a group home for teenagers in country New South Wales, where they'll receive counselling, education, support and love so they can regroup and move forward. Lisa inspires me every day by showing me what a whole lot of love, energy and hands-on work can achieve.

With Lisa's example in mind, I dug a little deeper and began to search for examples of women closer to home, whose achievements were a little more attainable, so the women I mentor could balance their reaching for the stars with grounded probability.

Similar stories were offered when I asked the women within my community who else inspires them. Which women do they come across in their everyday lives or in the wider community—sisters, friends, mothers, small-business owners—who are contributing to the world in a multitude of ways? These women can be flying under the radar in a world that so often celebrates the already famous, but as Pascale suggested, 'Those closer to us can have a greater impact because their achievements seem more attainable, more real.'

Sonja echoed this thought by saying, 'These women provide the hope, encouragement, contacts and support we need to have the courage and resilience to tread our own path and create our meaningful place in the world.'

There is no doubt that we all benefit from the power of example. The episodes on my podcast that receive the most comments are the wholehearted conversations I have with everyday women who share their stories of personal dreams becoming reality through focus, commitment, determination and heart. These stories open doors to new, achievable possibilities and provide the inspiration we need to pull us forward, helping us to create and take action on a new vision for ourselves.

The projects and work of these women are diverse in scope and style, but there is a clear, uniting thread that links them all. In most cases, they are strongly connected to a cause; they have a sense of purpose that aligns with their personal principles and beliefs. They are making a difference in the world in their own way, and we recognise, at a deep level, that's what we are here for as well. That's what *we* want, too.

It's never too late to change, to recognise discontent for what it is: an invitation.

You might hit a certain date on the calendar and experience a disquieting sense of pervasive panic as you look around and ask yourself, is this it? Is this all I have achieved in my life? Am I actually happy?

The opportunity nestled in that feeling of dismay is to expand your self-awareness, to notice when you're particularly prone to tripping over other people's achievements, and to learn to dance along the narrow ridge between inspiration and deflation.

Now is the time to recognise that you have everything you need to make new choices if you want to. And, most importantly, to understand that those choices need to be aligned with who you are and what's most important to you now. The flavour of your aspirations will always be unique to you, and way-showers can definitely become thought starters, rather than deflators, when you know how to take care of your own emotions. This practice is something I go into in more detail a little later in the book.

I can promise you that none of the women you admire woke up one magical morning with their plans perfectly laid out, with the media clamouring at their door, their hair coiffed, words of wisdom prepared, and their self-confidence wrapped around them like a familiar coat as they stepped out to wave, queen-like, to the waiting crowds. It's more likely that they felt a calling that simply would not go away; a calling that waited patiently as they dealt with the immediate demands of their lives. Then they began to respond to it, step by step, over time.

Maybe there was something in the beginning that made them curious, something fascinating that asked for their attention and eventually became irresistible. Or perhaps they had experienced a deep sense of disappointment, dismay or even outrage at something in their community or the world they could not accept any longer, and decided to take action, just imperfect action. Then they worked out their next steps, all the time moving forward. They were persistent. If one door shut, they opened another. If that door also closed, they found a window.

Brené Brown had to self-publish her first book because she couldn't get an agent, much less a publisher. 'I had hundreds of rejection letters. But I'm a very tenacious person, so I just outlasted failure.'[4]

When you understand that personal change, however, is an evolution, not a revolution, and that even the most seemingly effortless stories of success often have a back story of dogged determination and gradual growth, you will become emboldened to try.

THE CYCLE OF CHANGE

I've been fortunate to have worked with, interviewed, and collaborated with hundreds of women in my coaching and mentoring practice, and have reached many more through my podcast. These wholehearted conversations about life and dreams, businesses and challenges, successes and setbacks have helped me create a simple five-stage Cycle of Change model incorporating five distinctive steps that I see played out time and time again.

The Cycle of Change

The cycle of change is experienced in two distinct phases: 1) the deliberation phase, where your sense of discontent with what is, and your desire for what could be tussle with one another; and 2) the doing phase, where you're acting on your ideas, and designing and delivering your services, products and experiences to the world. The two phases are separated by a decision. It's simply not possible to take action in any significant, tangible way without the energy that comes from a clear and committed decision.

You'll move through the change cycle many times in your business and life as you and your ideas and passions evolve and grow, with new chapters emerging. And at every single stage of every single cycle you can expect to bump into doubt, fear, misbeliefs and uncertainty.

When I look back over my own life and consider how this model played out for me, two powerful and significant next-chapter moments stand out. They provide a stark before-and-after contrast, and both were born of my deep discontent with the circumstances I found myself in. This discontent was almost subconscious, and it grew in weight and impact over time until it reached a crescendo that crashed over me. Many people experience similar feelings just prior to significant change.

The first moment took place in 2006, but its origin was in the mid-eighties, when I was a teenager. As a teen, I tried so hard to fit in, but still managed to stand out in all the ways that adolescents abhor. There is a grab bag of examples I could pull from, but one in particular gouged itself into my heart, reverberating through my behaviour and self-image for many years.

I'd always been a swat at school. I studied hard, did well, was liked by teachers and dismissed by most of the cool crowd. I was also quite uncoordinated physically because of my poor eyesight, which meant I was always last to be picked for softball and netball teams, the key sports of the era. But then I discovered that I could run and, fortunately, you don't need twenty-twenty vision for that.

Athletics became my new favourite activity, and I could not have been more elated when, as a thirteen-year-old, one soaring leap into the long-jump pit nabbed me the gold medal at the North Island School Championships in New Zealand. This achievement capped off a fabulous year, which also included a few academic prizes, and I was practically bouncing with pride when I walked on stage in front of more than a thousand kids—until the hissing began.

The low hum of disapproval started somewhere in the middle of the assembly hall and was quickly picked up until it felt like the entire hall was alight with disapproval and rejection of me. My heart was thumping erratically. I could feel my pulse in my ears, deafening me. I disconnected from my body and yet somehow made it across the stage.

In that moment, all my suspicions about myself were confirmed. I was inherently *wrong*. I was flawed, utterly abhorrent.

This early experience of acute shame shaped me, defined me and, over time, almost broke me. I was completely reliant on my sense of self being delivered from an external source and was eager for approval and addicted to validation. When it was taken from me so cruelly, I was shattered, my confidence in pieces.

Unfortunately, what you look for, you find. What you focus on grows. That's the danger of relying on externally driven, and thus fragile, self-esteem instead of a strong, internally created foundation of self-worth. When your self-image feels eroded at the core, the pain of that disconnection can be so acute that your survival demands anaesthesia of some sort. In my case, I chose alcohol for my self-medication, and steely determination, achievement and approval for my self-esteem as I tried for many years to claw back validation and praise.

With this combination, I was able to soldier on and achieve many tick-the-box external goals and successes: a great career, marriage, children, and my own small business. But by my mid-thirties, the physical and emotional costs of maintaining the mask of confidence and achievement were starting to show.

My internal dialogue, delivered by a haughty comparison-queen inner critic was cruel and unrelenting: *You are useless, worthless, pointless and pathetic. Everyone is doing a better job than you.*

I believed what my inner critic told me, and I allowed my feelings of low self-worth, self-doubt and fear, along with a lack of value for who I was, to further disconnect me from any semblance of personal power. I was trapped in the cycle of being internally numbed by addiction and externally chained to a chameleon existence intended to ensure the approval of others.

I continued to search for answers, for an escape route. I knew in my heart that there had to be another way to live. Simple discontent had exploded into desperation, but I was exhausted and close to giving up. I'd explored all manner of options, ideas and cures to help me escape from the grip of my alcohol addiction. I went from the teeth-gritting, nail-biting agony of determined abstinence through sheer willpower, to visiting health farms, to undergoing sporadic counselling, to importing herbs and subliminal CDs that were 'guaranteed to free' me.

Nothing worked because I was never truly honest with myself. Shame wouldn't allow me to be.

While I did manage to maintain the roles of wife, mother and business owner, putting one foot in front of the other in a state known as high-functioning alcoholism, the colour had drained from my life. I was submerged in fear, unable to see a way out, and terrified that the cracks would begin to show in the careful facade I had in place. I felt sure that the world would soon see me as I really was.

Somehow, my story took a turn. One night in late 2006 I was alone in my home, my family asleep upstairs. I was in the bathroom, looking in the mirror, Groundhog Day nipping at my heels, my inner critic circling. For some reason, on this quiet night something shifted.

I remember it vividly. I saw myself—really *saw* myself—for the first time in as long as I could remember. I saw my pain clearly. I saw my sorrow. I saw my heart. And I softened for a moment. Just long enough for the thought to slip in that I could ask for help and possibly, just possibly, leave this deep, dark well of discontent behind.

I now know that the internal voice I connected with on that evening was a part of me I've learned to call the 'inner sage'. The inner sage is the essence of you. She is timeless. Patient. Loving. She is also discreet, and she is often hard to hear amid the noise, bluster and discouragement of our inner critic. Sometimes we need to let go to connect with her. We need to actually stop taking action and pause and listen.

That night, I was still and quiet enough to hear her.

I love the quote from JK Rowling that she shares when telling the story of her own remarkable change in fortune, which feels very apt when telling this story: 'Rock bottom became the solid foundation on which I rebuilt my life.'

Two weeks later I was in short-term rehab, beginning a twelve-step program that heralded an amazing new chapter of my life. I'm now in my fourteenth year of continuous recovery and have a completely revitalised mindset. Self-loathing has been replaced by self-compassion, an unconditional, supportive friendship with myself, and a deep appreciation of and reconnection to my unique unquestionable, boundless worth.

I have looked back at that night and sought to understand what primed me to unlock myself. I've come to realise that I had been given the keys to a new way of thinking and being by the power of an author who had shared her story, a story in which I could see myself. The book was *Drinking: A Love Story*. In this brave and powerful memoir, New York journalist Caroline Knapp chronicled her twenty years as a high-functioning alcoholic, and her awakening and journey back to life. Within the pages I witnessed how she had recognised her deep unhappiness and bottomless discontent, and had eventually found a way through.

I recently looked again at my well-worn copy of that book and felt great tenderness and compassion towards the younger me. She too had recognised her deep unhappiness and bottomless discontent, and underlined passages, scrawled intentions in the margins, and found hope within the pages. I celebrated how she eventually found her way out. I've often shared in recovery meetings that alcohol hijacked me, taking me off my path for several years, but I now am back again, on my way to becoming the woman I was always been meant to be.

Discontent served me well.

JUST BECAUSE YOU CAN, IT DOESN'T MEAN YOU SHOULD

My second turning point of discontent was in 2012. I had just arrived at the Sydney domestic airport to pick up my husband, who was returning after competing in the Sydney to Lord Howe Island Yacht Race.

Graham jumped into the car and tossed his sail bag onto the back seat. His eyes were shining, and he had a huge grin on his face. His excitement was palpable. 'It was incredible,' he said. 'Amazing! One night I was on evening watch and the sky was perfectly clear. The moon illuminated the ocean, and the water was shimmering. It was the most beautifully calm experience. The open ocean surrounded me for miles around. And then came the moment when the island came into sight on the horizon. It took my breath away.'

My husband was stepping into his own next chapter. A career of management consulting was giving way to the world of sailing and he had recently begun a business in the industry.

As he shared the excitement of his first offshore race, I could feel my own tension increasing. My heart was hammering in my chest, my stomach was in knots and I was finding it hard to breathe through the simmering resentment that was gripping me.

Finally, he turned to me and asked innocently, 'So, how was your week?'

I promptly burst into tears. Smacking my palms against the steering wheel in frustration, I cried, 'I just don't think I can do it anymore.'

I'd taken my marketing agency, Ideas into Action, from my dining-room table and built it into a thriving small business. I operated from an office on Sydney's North Shore, with a small team of full-time staff and fabulous suppliers. We were taking care of diverse clients across three states, enjoying increasing brand recognition in the market, and were generating that magical multiple six figures per annum in revenue.

I had ticked so many success boxes, and I didn't understand why I felt so distressed, exhausted, and utterly, miserably discontented.

Perhaps I would have seen this outburst just waiting to take centre stage if I'd looked a little closer at my life: my reliance on cigarettes and energy drinks, the crazy juggle of before- and after-school care, the late nights and early mornings, the trying to be all things to all people, including best mother, wife, employer and business owner. My life was so busy that there was little time left for me.

I'd been pushing down my discontent for so long, stuck in the narrative that the grind of hard work was the only path to success. So when Graham put his hand over mine and said quietly, 'Then don't,' I looked at him in disbelief.

Surely it wasn't that simple.

While Graham was so joyfully embracing the next chapter of his career, I was wading through immense confusion and unhappiness in my own, even though outwardly it looked good by the typical measures of success.

Following what the world says you should follow may look good on the outside, without matching your needs or deep desire for purpose and meaning on the inside. Achievement doesn't guarantee happiness, contentment or fulfilment. My truth was that I'd built a business that utilised my skills, but no longer reflected my values, engaged my heart or truly reflected the woman I had become. I was beginning to understand that just because I could, it didn't mean I should, and that life was too short not to be doing the work in the world I was truly here for. I knew another change was coming.

With the help of some simple and powerful tools, I finally made the choice to close the business, let go of my staff, and shift from business consulting to mentoring, inspiring and supporting other women. These days I understand that a sustainable business is one that blends contribution, fulfilment and financial reward, and allows me the flexibility to fit the business around my life. That's what I now have in this chapter, and I delight in helping other women appreciate the value of their own unique experience and insights, trust their intuition, and realign their business vision and services with their values and not just their skills.

But I had to move all the way through several levels of discontent until I became uncomfortable enough to make this change.

THE DISCONTENT CONTINUUM

Since you're reading this book, I'm sure you're familiar with the feeling of discontent, but do you know where you sit on the continuum? I have experienced the symptoms of discontent, and seen them in others, and I know they tend to deepen over time.

Read through this list to see where you fall on the continuum:

- Irritable: It's difficult to put your finger on it, but you know something is not right.
- Contemplative: You spend a great deal of time imagining a different career, a different life, but don't invest any time in acting on these fantasies.
- Comparative: You're pressing your nose to the windows of other people's businesses and lives, disappearing down an internet rabbit hole, and feeling a mixture of envy and despair.
- Yearning: You often find yourself pausing and gazing into the distance, sighing. Then you square your shoulders and get on with things.

- Trapped and resentful: You complete tasks with an edge of anger that you manage to keep contained most of the time. The quality of your work is often the victim here.
- Resignation: You feel flat and listless, and entirely without motivation, but you're resigned to your fate, believing there are no alternatives for you.
- Desperate: You feel overwhelmed and breathless, even slightly manic, as you contemplate everything you have to do while realising that you have no real desire to do any of it.

How do you know when you're off course? You begin to notice a growing sense of restlessness and irritation, possibly accompanied by a lingering sense of sadness. At the heart of discontentment is unexpressed potential. You're both distracted and contemplative because something inside you is asking to be seen.

You need to respond; you need to explore; you need to look more closely at what this emotion is trying to show you. Discontent can transform into possibility when it's given its head to roam and question.

Awareness of the need for change can creep up slowly and gradually, tapping you on the shoulder and quietly asking for your attention every now and then. It can also hit suddenly and powerfully, appearing out of the blue, making you gasp for air with its ferocity, as it did for me that afternoon. The end result is the same, no matter the route.

You begin to understand that ignoring your sense of discontent is a form of self-sabotage because it means you've been settling for less than you can achieve. You've been caged, and your full view of the world obscured.

What used to satisfy you and fill you up has been replaced by hunger, an appetite for more than what is already on your plate and in your life.

This feeling of dissatisfaction can actually invoke a sense of guilt in you. It's as though you believe there's something inherently wrong with reaching the edge of satisfaction and wanting to expand, almost as though you're being disloyal to those around you, the people you love. You may scold yourself and ask what right you have to feel dissatisfied with your life. You tell yourself to look at all that you have.

Your sense of guilt may be met with resistance and justification. Looking at your life and counting your blessings is when the 'yes, but' and 'should' and 'shouldn't' make their presence known:

- I really shouldn't want more than what I already have.
- Yes, this might not be lighting me up, but it's good work and I should appreciate it.
- Yes, I feel completely crappy, but it's paying the bills and I should be grateful.
- Yes, I might want to do it, but right now this has to be enough.
- Yes, I might not love it, but really, what right do I have to complain?

This strange sense of floating guilt is often compounded by self-doubt, accompanied by negative thoughts:

- Yes, I might dream about it, but what chance is there of me doing *that*, really?
- Who am I to think that I can have more, that I can create something different?
- If I haven't made it by now I never will.

- It's been done before.
- It's too late.
- I'm too old.
- It would never work anyway.
- Even if I tried, I'm not likely to be very successful.
- I won't be able to make any money doing what I really want to do.

These strong and challenging thoughts can result in an almost automatic shutdown of ambition and expansion, keeping you stuck unless you shine the light of awareness on them. You're entitled to own your discontent, to recognise it as a symbol of the next chapter that's asking for your attention.

And self-doubt? I've not yet come across a woman who doesn't have this emotion as a faithful companion during any worthwhile endeavour. It's keeping me company through almost every page of writing this book. The key is to see and acknowledge the doubt and then choose to move forward regardless, holding on tight to the understanding that action is the antidote to fear; no one can ever change without walking along their personal growth edges.

THE ROLE OF RESISTANCE

Resistance is another reaction to the feeling of discontent, and it can be confronting to acknowledge it. It's far easier to dismiss it, suppress it, and turn away, even when you know it's telling you the truth: that you're being restricted. Why would you resist moving through an emotion that stifles you? Wouldn't you logically want to traverse this territory and come out the other side?

You resist it because you're human. You know that when you step fully into discontent, when you actually face it and all the revelations it brings with it, it's going to be confrontational. Resistance has regret riding shotgun, linked to the choices you've made or haven't made in your life that have brought you to this point.

When you take a closer look at your sense of regret you might feel that you should've turned left at some point in your past instead of right, and that such a choice would have delivered a much better outcome. Dancing at the edges of your imagination is the belief that different choices might have created new possibilities for opening up your life. These are the thoughts that visit at three in the morning and taunt you with their what-ifs. They're painful.

Conversely, you could experience a sense of relief, believing that your careful and considered choices have kept you safe and on a straight path, with a world of potential disasters averted. Initially that can feel quite satisfying. You often reach the stage of your life, however, when you have the space and opportunity for deeper reflection, leading to a pervasive sense that you have missed out by playing safe.

You might wonder if you would have experienced much more if you'd had the courage to take chances. Such sliding-door moments can leave you with a sense of regret, sorrow for what might have been, and lingering sadness at lost potential. And who wants to spend time in such a place?

If that's the flavour of your discontent, the key is to allow these feelings the space they need. This is pivotal for future ease.

One thing I've learned in my own experience of navigating the gap between what is now and what has been is to allow myself to feel the phantom pain, the wistfulness, melancholy and even anger that can be associated with the sense of perceived lost possibilities. It's only when I fully explore these feelings, giving them the space they need to be seen and heard regardless of the sadness this may entail, that I can let go and move on.

In the recovery community we talk about the need to 'feel, deal, heal'. Trying to push down feelings of sadness, regret, resentment and anger takes a ton of energy. And even if you do manage to hold these feelings down now, they will eventually resurface in some other area, often at the most inopportune time, accompanied by a tremendous amount of pushback energy that can knock you flat or even damage a relationship.

YOUR EMOTIONAL VOCABULARY

There are two practices I'd like to introduce you to that will enable you to recognise, welcome and work with discontent, understanding that those things are simply signposts for change and a new expression of you. They help me work through feelings, especially uncomfortable ones, harvest the lessons, let go and regain a sense of emotional equilibrium.

The first practice involves improving your emotional literacy with an expanded vocabulary. The second practice involves conducting a personal inventory.

The ability to recognise and own what you're feeling in a given moment is the centrepiece of emotional health. This gift of insight will lessen your chances of being hijacked by your emotions. Instead, it will allow you to respond mindfully, and to make appropriate, informed choices. To make plans and then take aligned, supportive action.

As you examine your newly discovered discontent and the feelings underpinning it, your emotional literacy will help you feel calmer and more in control. You will be able to understand your reactions. Having a more accurate, thorough picture of what you're feeling means you're far more able to do something about it.

There is a huge difference between feeling irritated and feeling furious, between feeling disappointed and feeling inconsolable, and between feeling doubt and feeling shame. The distinctions between emotions—the nuances that we can grasp and articulate—make a real difference.

When you are clearer on what you're experiencing, you can also be clearer on how to respond. Feeling sorrow and shame asks for a more compassionate response than feeling a smidgen of guilt. The first may reveal the need for professional, compassionate support while the second could be addressed with a simple apology.

The judgmental combination of frustration and envy that can be triggered when we see what someone is doing with their business can be a clear clue that we really want to be doing something similar.

There are many lists of emotions that can be found with a simple online search. One of my favourite lists is from Byron Katie, a freely accessible download associated with her website, The Work of Byron Katie.[5] She not only helps you to pinpoint your emotions, but also challenges you to consider who you could be without the thoughts that cling to them.

I encourage you to work with your emotions by creating a habit of checking in with yourself a few times during the day. Simply pause, look inside and ask: *How am I feeling?* Take the first emotion that presents itself and challenge yourself to dig a little deeper. Is that your best description? Is there a more expansive, more accurate emotion you can identify? Ask yourself what your response is trying to tell you.

All emotions have purpose. None need to be avoided. If it sometimes feels like you're caught in the fire, there can be great power and great comfort in knowing that whatever emotion you are experiencing, it will pass. Allow it. Feel it. Deal with it. Then you can make informed choices; you can heal and grow.

CONDUCTING A PERSONAL INVENTORY

This exercise helps you to identify, examine and release the fears, resentments and negative thoughts that often come to the surface when you commit to becoming more aware of your emotions. Discontent has a myriad of feelings hidden beneath it that are tied to personal beliefs and specific experiences that, when identified, examined and released, can set you free to step forward.

I was first exposed to this practice in the 12-step work that was a cornerstone to my recovery. It was illuminating and empowering, and I continue to use it in my everyday life.

Start by drawing up five columns, either in your journal or on a piece of paper, and head them up as follows:

Column 1: Person, place or thing
Column 2: Describe the situation
Column 3: How does this make me feel?
Column 4: What part have I played in this situation?
Column 5: What is the cost to me (how does it hold me back)?

In the first column, list the people or situations that create fear, anxiety or resentment in you. The following prompts may help you come up with ideas:

- What am I afraid of?
- What do I feel resentful of?
- What am I sad about?
- What do I feel regret for?
- What am I anxious about?

In the second column, briefly describe the situation that has created these feelings in you.

In the third column, note how the situation makes you feel. What emotions are rising to the surface? What does it make you think, feel and say to yourself?

In the fourth column, ask yourself what part you have played. Have you helped to create it? Growth is not possible without taking a high degree of personal responsibility. When you are honest with yourself you might see that lethargy, an outdated perspective, or even a tangible, regrettable action has contributed to the current situation. This discovery can be both confronting and liberating, and reveal what you can now do to grow.

In the fifth column, identify what this is costing you. How is it feeding your sense of discontent? Is it creating fear and holding you back in your life today?

Your table will look something like this:

Person, place or thing	Describe the situation	How does this make me feel?	What part have I played in this?	What is the cost to me (how is it holding me back)?
Diane	She's published a book that's already had more than 8000 downloads on Amazon.	Envious, frustrated, inferior, pessimistic. I'll never enjoy that level of success. I'm not nearly good enough so why should I even bother trying?	I'm watching every move she makes and comparing myself to her. I haven't started my own book yet, even though I've wanted to for a long time.	I don't even try. I have an idea for a book, but I don't think it's worth writing. All I do is procrastinate and berate myself. I waste so much energy, and the negative feelings impact my other work.
Stephanie	She never listens to me. She always has a bigger, better story to tell and dominates every conversation we have.	Angry, resentful, closed. She never has time for me and is too focused on herself.	I don't call her very often. She probably feels that she needs to fit everything into the conversation.	A strained relationship. I'm always feeling guilty or angry and that stops me from calling; it's a vicious circle.

Can you see how reactions and thoughts create feelings? Recurring thoughts like this can create a downward spiral and are certainly not conducive to emotional equilibrium and forward progress.

Your initial challenge is to get all of your top-of-mind thoughts, feelings and fears associated with your sense of discontent into this list and look for patterns. It's the repeat offenders that you want to identify and release. You could share these with a close friend to help articulate and release them. This is a key part of the step work we do in recovery. With a compassionate listener—someone who, as Brené Brown says, 'has earned the right to hear your story'—it can be an incredibly freeing process.

Since my own first formal foray into this practice I've found that simply discovering and acknowledging my feelings and then discarding the notes to be effective. Releasing them to a higher power, and asking for help in removing any doubts, fears or other emotional states that are holding you back, is also a powerful symbolic exercise.

If there is a lot of emotion that comes to the surface when you're working through this inventory, and there often is, you may need to seek professional help.

I'm grateful to have found a counsellor who helps me to untangle my emotions when they threaten to get the better of me. I also have a support circle of businesswomen who help me remove the obstacles that I tend to place on my own path forward.

You may also like to explore a spiritual solution. One such example I love is the Hawaiian healing philosophy ho'oponopono,[6] a simple and powerful four-step release mantra encompassing these phrases:

1. I'm sorry.
2. Please forgive me.
3. Thank you.
4. I love you.

Make friends with your discontent. I trust you can now see that it is not something to be pushed aside or held down. Rather, open your arms wide and welcome it in. Offer it a seat. Get to know it. Appreciate the message it brings. Consider the invitation it hands you. Take a breath and allow it to introduce you to your next visitor: desire.

'Every great dream begins with a dreamer. You have within you the strength, the patience, and the passion to reach for the stars and change the world.'

Harriet Tubman

CHAPTER 2

DESIRE

Explore What's Calling You

When I was growing up on a small farm in New Zealand, I spent hours constructing elaborate mountain ranges out of the thick quilt from my parents' bed for my menagerie of plastic animals to live in. The bedding was heavy enough to fall in interesting ways, creating the caves, ridges, peaks and valleys that allowed my imagination to roam freely as I wove tales of pursuit and escape, and magic and mayhem with the characters I created.

My mother has told me that I used to disappear into these worlds for hours at a time. She'd stand at the door watching me, fascinated by the dozens of different voices I used as I gave each creature its own part to play in the landscapes I created. I remember these games clearly and I love the memories of my playful, exuberant self.

I also remember the day when I sat down to play and found that the desire to do so had gone. I'd crossed the threshold that divided childhood from the next stage of my life, and it was time for new interests and desires.

As an adult, it's been interesting to reflect on that stage of my life and notice how I didn't fight the feeling. I didn't try to force myself into a shape that didn't fit me anymore. I didn't fret and agonise over what was going to replace my old fascinations. I just accepted what was true for me then. I knew intuitively that all I needed to do was let go and trust that the next thing meant for me would arrive soon, and that I would recognise it when it did.

I think it might have been roller skates.

TRUSTING YOURSELF

As grown women, how do we tap into that sense of trust we had as children, of knowing what's right for us from the inside out? We all had access to that innate knowledge when we were young. There was no judgment, no evaluation. We felt with our whole selves, responded openly and chose spontaneously. Even if we subsequently changed our minds, we did so without concern. We discarded what didn't align anymore and set off to discover what did. Curiosity, wonder, joy and awe guided us then and I believe they still can now, if we allow them to.

So, how do we unpack and understand desire? How do we pin down this often-elusive understanding of ourselves? How can we find our true path in life? How do we even connect with what we really want when we may feel out of touch with ourselves, or even at a complete loss when it comes to describing that part of ourselves?

The popular notion that if you do what you love you'll never work a day in your life sounds seductive and enticing, but it's also a little misleading. Your sense of purpose, just like you, evolves over time, and effort is definitely required to connect with it. It takes effort to first notice and then acknowledge that you have fledgling desires. And it takes effort to catch hold of that wisp of interest, and begin to explore what it is and what it means when you don't have a map nicely laid out in front of you to guide your journey.

I believe that the concept of being 'on purpose', of finding that one true thing that we're here for has been responsible for tying too many of us in knots. The definition of one true thing is too narrow, too precise and too restrictive, and it places a whole lot of pressure on our shoulders. How can we be confined to one thing when we're packed to our core with years of experience, appetites, interests, uncertainties, fears and doubts?

I believe you are here, on this planet, in this life, to self-actualise. I believe it is your absolute, unassailable right to keep correcting your course until you find yourself in the territory of your truth, where you can stumble across or tenaciously uncover delight. You can then explore and expand what lights you up, and choose to immerse yourself in the projects, crafts, hobbies and work that have deep meaning for you.

I think of this as living, working, loving, contributing purposefully, rather than finding and wholly committing to a single purpose.

People who focus their unique talents in ways that feel purposeful and have meaning for them feel valuable, useful and inspired. They are strongly connected to their self-worth and confident of the value they create. As a result, they contribute to the world at their full capacity, with enthusiasm, generosity and joy. They support causes, start businesses, launch charities, create products, become volunteers, get behind community initiatives, and fully involve themselves in all manner of endeavours that serve them just as much as they serve the world.

It's a win-win arrangement, the symbiosis that is the essence of self-actualisation and moves the whole world forward. We want and need more people who are fully committed to their desires, people who are energised and passionate, who are the best versions of themselves because they're doing what they're designed to do.

KNOWING WHAT YOU WANT

We often ask ourselves searching questions: *What do I truly want to create? What can I contribute? What is it that I'm good at? What's my calling?* We sometimes dig deep, urgently searching for answers that will perhaps sweep across the globe and leave an impact that will go down in history. While I am a big dreamer, I've also become aware that positive impact is a rolling stone, gathering momentum over time. I agree with the wisdom of Stephen Covey, author of *The 7 Habits of Highly Successful People*,[7] when he tells us to 'begin with the end in mind', but I'm also cautious about setting the bar for a vision so high that it feels disconnected from possibility.

I want you to feel your desires, to fully inhabit them, to have them beating a consistent rhythm in your heart every day, right within your grasp. As your confidence and self-belief grow, as you gather more and more evidence of your capability, you can extend those desires, unfurl them so they expand across your sky.

I'm not suggesting that you forgo seeking to positively impact the world, on the contrary. I have no doubt that if the collective talents of women, much of which is currently untapped, were harnessed and directed outwards, the world would shake with our power. I realise that replacing the often-bandied-about directive 'dream big' with 'dream medium' is unlikely to catch on with a wider audience, but I still advocate for this because it allows room for you to breathe. To shape your desires as you move, to not wait until they're perfectly formed before you act upon them.

I've found that this more measured approach can counter the tendency to feel elated one day and overwhelmed the next. You don't want to feel frustrated, bewildered or lost at this early stage in your new development. Feeling you need specificity, or that you're pinned under the depth and breadth of the need for a massive vision, can stifle and drown out the quiet voice inside that wants to be heard.

Your dreaming self can also be buried under the demands of your day-to-day responsibilities and obligations. You might find yourself working in or running the business that suits your capabilities rather than the business you *want* to work in, often as a result of happenstance rather than conscious choice or deliberate design.

That was my story with my marketing agency, until I realised where I had landed and allowed my dreaming self a voice again. The invitation is always there for you to change your current reality, in ways large and small, when you recognise that you've stepped through your own threshold. Even if you feel you've lost touch with what you want, or doubt your ability to find a new desire, I promise you that under those layers of uncertainty or doubt your heart is ready to connect to deep meaning. You just need to tease out that meaning gently.

CREATING YOUR OWN MAP

To navigate towards the sweet spot where contribution, fulfilment and financial reward intersect for you, you'll need the twin wheels of discontent and joy.

How do you know if you're off course? You'll find yourself on the discontent continuum we explored earlier, feeling lost, irritated, resigned or even desperate for change. When you experience sustained discontent, even when your situation is seemingly great, it means that something more is coming, something else is just over the horizon.

To bring that something into focus you need to start with a counterintuitive strategy. Rather than immediately trying to define what could be next for you, a challenge that can leave you feeling pressured and floundering, you need to start with a different goal.

The first step is to become aware of what you *don't* want. This knowledge will help you more easily define the territory of your next chapter. So, grab your journal and a pen, and begin to identify what's no longer interesting or desirable for you. Recognise when it's time to put away your own menagerie of plastic animals.

Make a list of things you *don't* want. I've listed a few possibilities to get you started:

- I don't want to work nine-to-five days.
- I don't want to feel lost when the kids move away.
- I don't want to travel so much and be away from my family.
- I don't want to write marketing plans for others.
- I don't want to offer one-on-one services.

- I don't want to have the responsibility of staff.
- I don't want to do this alone anymore.
- I don't want to work for anyone else.
- I don't want to do work that doesn't feel like it matters.

All you need to do to get started is flip these statements and list the things you *do* want instead. Become a detective in your own life and search for evidence of joy. Recall the times when you've felt a little more interested, a little happier, a smidgen more energised. A few possibilities:

- I want the flexibility to set my own working hours.
- I want to tap into my creativity again.
- I want a short commute each day.
- I want to run workshops and teach business owners how to write their own plans.
- I want to fly solo, with no staff and no office.
- I want more collaboration, maybe even a business partner.
- I want to work for myself.
- I want to contribute to a particular cause and use my time to make a difference.

Expect to see more desires tiptoeing into the picture as you work through this process, almost as though they sense that you're opening up and they feel safe to be seen. Welcome them, catch them, and get them down on paper. There's no need to evaluate them at this stage; you just need to acknowledge that they've arrived. Now you can begin to use these two contrasting lists to guide you, to hone your internal compass.

You can start the process by moving away from what feels heavy, discouraging or simply boring. Do fewer of those things.

Your awareness of what isn't feeling good to you now, at this stage of your life, will nudge you gently in the direction of what feels better. Do more of those things.

And when pure joy occasionally dashes into view, quickly turn towards it. Ask yourself what stirred it up. What did you see, hear, or experience that created it?

For me, this process was the starting point. I began to become ready to let go of the restrictions that my agency, with its 8am–6pm hours, demanded of me. Did you notice how I said 'began to become ready'? This process is part of the evolution I mentioned earlier. The trumpets, parting clouds and purpose-etched stone tablet I dreamed of are seldom the reality, so allow yourself the space and grace for exploration and gradual honing, for becoming ready.

The better you understand yourself, the easier it will be to trust yourself, to listen to your intuition.

I found that exploring a number of personality-style tests was fun and an interesting way to further enhance my self-awareness and self-knowledge as I explored what my own next chapters would entail. In particular, the Instinctive Drives methodology[8] created by Paul Burgess helped me appreciate why I thrive when I can inspire others to move through uncharted territory and expand in ways they didn't think were possible.

The insights from this test are still inspiring me to connect to my natural strengths and internal desires more deeply, which means I can develop my next project in alignment with who I am at a deep level.

ENDING OLD STORIES

On a recent call with my counsellor I shared a breakthrough moment that was the result of deep reflection. One of my habits has often been to make quick decisions. It can certainly be a strength—I don't get stuck in procrastination, and I can make things happen pretty quickly once I set my mind to them—but like all things in life there's also a flip side to this skill. I can sometimes find myself regretting the results of my fast-action decisions, wishing I'd given myself permission to pause, and the space to consider my options.

I recently managed to do exactly that, and I was delighted at what I'd discovered. The reflection I'd gifted myself with had allowed me to see that I was carrying the remnants of an old story around with me that was discolouring my present.

In this story, I was sure I should be living a more flamboyant life. How I was living and working was just not exciting enough, not big enough or bold enough. It was a subscription-style belief, delivered on a regular basis by my comparison-queen inner critic who told me I should desire a particular version of adventure, freedom and wildness. My comparison queen had me noticing (typically via social media) what other people were up to and wanted me to feel inadequate and small. Boring. She often succeeded and exerted a destabilising influence on me, knocking me off my own course.

But I'd managed to peel off another layer to reach a deeper sense of awareness. I'd begun to see that this story didn't fit me now, and in fact never had. I'm simply not the flamboyant gypsy type and that's perfectly okay. I don't need to automatically dive headfirst into activities I see others sharing that look exciting or impressive on the surface, either in my business or my personal life. Doing so without checking in and seeing if they actually fit me at a deeper level would mean I would ultimately end up unhappy, because these things really are not for me.

I realised that the things I love, and the way that I want to live and work, are perfect for me, even though it may mean a quieter and simpler life. I now know there is no need for me to apologise to my inner critic for not wanting to be someone other than who I am.

I stepped out of the story that wasn't mine. I had borrowed that story back when I didn't know who I was. It was an outdated reference, a false identity that had ceased to be a desirable destination. I didn't want or need to go there anymore.

The freedom that came from that simple realisation, from discarding the story that I'm not enough and that my natural desires are not scintillating enough, was utterly liberating. I'm comfortable in my own skin today. I can continue to focus on shaping the life and business that actually aligns with me, rather than chasing after a celebrated ideal, some formula or solution that isn't actually a fit at all. The decisions I now make from this place of acceptance and wholeness are more likely to be considered, rather than compulsive. They're strong, clear and expansive.

LISTENING INSIDE

I encourage you to take time to consider the narrative that you might be caught in that could be influencing you regarding the choices you make. This can make it difficult for you to recognise your true desires, independent of what you've been subtly conditioned to believe, or told outright that you should want. Your inner sage knows. But she needs space, peace and quiet to allow that knowing to float up into your consciousness.

When I asked the women around me how they tap into their desires and become clear on what they want, they shared similar sentiments.

Kirana: 'I have a very clear feeling about that in my body, something which feels very different to an intellectual decision or even a want. I can only describe it as *I know*, as in a deep inner knowledge.'

Donna: 'I rely on meditation, channelling and imagining, supported by intuition and body feedback and guidance.'

Lynne: 'I have my own version of a SWOT analysis that I call "the four L's". Instead of strengths, weaknesses, opportunities and threats, I list the types of work and activities that I love, like, can live with, and loathe. The answers help me identify what I want (and don't want) to do, not just what I'm good at doing.'

Leanne: 'I think it's harder to be clear when there's lots of clutter. Getting away from the noise seems to be where the answers come from. I also find I see recurring ideas or feelings pop up again and again until I finally listen or take notice.'

The reference that Leanne makes to recurring ideas and feelings is particularly important. One of the most common phrases I hear when I'm working with women is: *There's this idea that I've had for so long ...*

When something lingers, when it just won't go away, when it continually taps you quietly on the shoulder, please give it your attention. If it has staying power, it usually means it really does deserve an audience and consideration. It often needs to be set free from any old stories about why it won't work, especially if you've tried to develop it in the past but had to let it go because the timing wasn't right.

When I closed my business, Ideas Into Action, in 2012, initially I wanted nothing to do with marketing and business strategy. I was done. I renamed myself a 'self-worth mentor', utterly convinced by my own experience that this was what the world needed.

Back then it was a challenge for me to explain what worthiness was and why it was so essential for growth and actualisation. The mentors I had around me at the time were quite dismissive of the concept, telling me that no one was searching for self-worth, and that I couldn't build a business around such a notion.

I listened. I acquiesced, and changed tack, developing a more palatable message that nevertheless evolved over time into the form I share today: stepping into your next chapter. I love my work. I adore the clients I work with and the services I've chosen to deliver. But the desire to fully embody the message of the value of women reconnecting to their self-worth, and to share the practices and tools I've found most useful, has never left me. I have incorporated it into the foundations of my business mentoring work, but with the volume turned down. It has sat in the background for years, patiently waiting for me to give it the full attention it deserves, which is now.

As I've navigated my own cycle of change yet again, I've chosen to bring the importance of self-worth out of the shadows, to discard the narrative of 'you can't lead with that' that was given to me in the past, and to give my message full voice in a new project and an emerging body of work, The Self-Worth Institute, that will sit alongside my core business programs.

Through the institute I'll be providing a Facilitators Certification Program for leaders, coaches, trainers, wellness advocates, and other professionals. The tools and practices I'll share will help to anchor their clients, colleagues, teams and communities in self-worth, ensuring their own programs and services are then able to be more fully absorbed and actioned. My fledging vision will evolve into a full expression of a desire I have been waiting to welcome into my world for quite some time.

Do you have your own slumbering desire that's been waiting for its time in the sun? Perhaps you can unpack it and look at it again with fresh eyes.

Your desires can be rekindled simply by being in motion, by following the breadcrumbs of experiences. I encourage you to pay attention to situations where positive feelings and enjoyment naturally emerge. When you realise you're in flow, what you're doing becomes easy and fluid.

Become curious and look closely at where you are and what you're doing. You might see a piece of your own puzzle falling into place. Perhaps it won't be the whole picture, and that's utterly fine. If it's just the next step, that's enough. You can take that next step. You can step out in faith without knowing exactly where it's leading you because this stage of your next chapter is all about curiosity and exploration.

THE POWER OF WAY-SHOWERS

I first came across the concept of way-showers—literally, people who show the way to what's possible—when I was interviewing Barbara Huson (nee Stanny) on my podcast. The bestselling author of several books, including *Overcoming Underearning* and *Sacred Success*, she focuses her message on sharing her path to financial independence, inspiring countless women to become smarter with money.

Barbara and I discussed the importance of having a community of support around you, especially when you're expanding in new directions. At this stage of the Your Next Chapter change cycle, it can be helpful to observe role models, either close to you or far away. Be aware of the examples that intrigue and delight you, that captivate your imagination. These are all signs, possible breadcrumbs to follow into your future. They provide powerful proof of what aligning with your desires and living a full and authentic life really mean, showing you that it's possible for you, too.

Brené Brown is another of my way-showers. I discovered her first book, *I Thought It Was Just Me (But It Isn't)*, early in my recovery journey. Curled up on a seat in my lounge room, with lightning bolts of recognition blasting through my body, I was riveted by her story. I delighted in the notion that my experience of not being enough was almost certainly universal and definitely not fatal.

The seed of desire to share my own story to help unlock other women, which was already planted in my heart, shivered. It seemed to take up a little more space. At that stage, I wasn't ready to respond to the tiny, emerging desire to move away from my agency business model into something that was more aligned with the woman I was becoming. But I was becoming more aware of the possibility. It was beginning to take form in my heart and mind.

FOLLOW YOUR FLEDGLING DESIRES

Albert Einstein told us that 'imagination is more important than knowledge', a belief that will serve you well. You need to play with an idea in the theatre of your mind before you can bring it to life in the real world. The desire to create is a strong source of inspiration, and it will pull you forward, often far more effectively than the push of motivation. The *why* of your desire deserves more focus than the *how*; it is how you will overcome any inertia that has possibly left too many great ideas in the too-hard basket.

When you see other women accomplishing something that stirs you, it's a sign that you may need to examine something a little more closely. Perhaps you notice a particular shopfront and feel the tug of a wish in your heart. Or you see a post on social media from someone who's launching something new and you catch your breath. That's a message. Take note.

Several years ago, I was in the audience at an entrepreneurial event in Las Vegas with two good friends and fellow businesswomen when a new desire fluttered to life in my chest. It was exhilarating to be surrounded by purposeful women who were sharing their dreams and intentions out loud and being met with encouragement and support. In that space, I felt that anything was achievable. I wanted to stay in the atmosphere, soaking up the energy of possibility.

In that moment I decided to do the next best thing: to anchor myself in the desire to recreate the experience back in Australia. I had no idea how I would manage this, and when I returned home I had to find my way through a whole field of doubts to transform the desire into reality. Your Next Chapter Live was the result, an event I've held twice. The desire that appeared and curled up on my lap as I sat in the audience that day knew it belonged to me.

When this happens to you, when a fledging desire arrives and takes your hand, allow yourself to dance down that road of imagination; the desire is letting you know that it wants to be adopted. Accept the invitation, catch hold of the notion and work with it. You might find yourself reading an article and feel a rising sense of outrage or injustice, and a desire to *do something* about the issue. This is also a sign, a clue. Don't ignore it. Explore it.

Grab your journal and answer these questions:

- I've always wanted to ...
- When I see women do ... I feel ...
- When I was younger, I always thought I would ...
- When I read stories about ... I feel ...
- The issue that really riles me is ...
- When I allow myself to dream with no limits, I think I might ...
- I've noticed that ... keeps coming up for me when ...
- I feel I'm at my best when I'm ...

Think of desire as a wee spark, the essence of an idea that will flare when it's nurtured and given air to breathe. Are you ready to act on what you discover?

For some of us, our desires are obvious. They're clear and compelling. We nurture a dream and pursue it single-mindedly and with determination and clarity. If that's been you, bravo, I celebrate you and the beautiful example you provide for all of us. This may also have been you in the past before life took you off on a detour. And perhaps that original compelling vision you had has faded somewhat and it needs your attention for it to ignite again.

Or you may be someone whose vision was strong, and the actions you took focused and successful. But now you find yourself standing atop your own personal mountain of achievement that no longer provides the satisfaction it once did. If this is you, you may need to regroup and tap into a new level and direction of desire.

Perhaps it never occurred to you until now that you wanted other than what you actually have. The yearning that has sat quietly in the background has asserted itself and asked for your attention. And perhaps now you have recognised your discontent and are allowing yourself to explore your desires.

It doesn't matter what has brought you to this point. It's only important to know that you are here, that you are in transition, that you are not alone as a life re-designer, and that you only need a few simple ingredients to begin to create a new recipe, unique to you. Those ingredients are curiosity, contribution, honesty and joy.

You're ready for your next chapter, you're in the middle of the cycle of change, and the signposts are pointing to a transformation that you can now direct, a transformation that's as much internal as it is external.

Follow your heart. You've got this.

'We all have our own life to pursue, our own kind of dream to be weaving, and we all have the power to make wishes come true, as long as we keep believing.'

Louisa May Alcott

CHAPTER 3

DOUBT

A Passenger on Every Voyage

In 2015, I polled the women in my community, asking them what was holding them back from bringing their next-chapter business dreams to life. Almost ninety percent of the respondents gave the same answer: *Me. I am.* This is just a sample of what they shared with me:

- I don't have belief in my skills or myself.
- I know I could achieve more, but I need to trust myself more to do that.
- I struggle with procrastination and self-confidence.
- I find it difficult to have faith in myself, to know I'm as good as everyone else in my field.
- I am my own worst enemy.
- I have a terrible case of perfectionism paralysis.

- I have a very hard time writing, and when I do, I'm critical and don't want the world to see it.
- My self-doubt is crippling me; I'm constantly comparing myself to others and to other businesses.
- I don't believe I can actually make money doing what I love.
- I'm scared of failing, of making a fool of myself.
- I'm scared that my idea, or myself, won't be good enough.
- I know I have low self-esteem.
- I doubt that I can really do this.
- I self-sabotage by keeping busy with other things instead of prioritising my business.
- I lack belief in myself, my skills, my experience and knowledge, even though I've had some wonderful experiences lately that have shown me that there's no reason not to believe in myself.
- My self-confidence is very low.
- I have nothing original to say or contribute; it's all been done before.
- My story is not going to be inspiring for anyone.
- I'm not ready yet.
- I don't have qualifications so I can't be successful.

On the one hand, these results could be seen as refreshing; they indicate that most of the stumbling blocks these women encountered were not external. But how frustrating it is to try to build a beautiful business and make a difference in the world while being simultaneously strangled by thoughts and misbeliefs like these. I wondered if the women in my community were just having a down day, maybe going through a difficult patch when they completed the survey, or whether this problem was more widespread.

When I looked deeper into the subject, I discovered that over the past twenty years research on the impact of gender and age on self-belief has played a prominent role in psychology. A confidence gender gap emerges in adolescence and continues throughout early and middle adulthood.

While men tend to overestimate their abilities and performance, women tend to underestimate both. An internal report at Hewlett-Packard revealed that women apply for open jobs only if they think they meet a hundred percent of the criteria listed, while men apply if they believe they meet only sixty percent of the requirements.[9] Further evidence of this confidence gap is seen with men initiating salary negotiations four times as often as women, and with women asking for thirty percent less money than men.[10]

I see a similar trend in the entrepreneurial world. Clients will provide their insights and services freely during complimentary discussions, but often become uncomfortable and uncertain when it comes to presenting their fees.

At my live events I asked the women to close their eyes and raise their hands if the thoughts I uncovered in my community survey were a part of their inner dialogue. There was not a woman in the room who did not have her hand up. In fact, they all had both hands up and several said that they needed to raise their feet as well.

If this is how you feel—how you *truly* feel when the walls come down and you're honest with yourself—how are you going to act on your desire for change? If, no matter how good your ideas, or how passionate you feel about them, self-doubt keeps getting in the way; if fear quietens your voice; if misbeliefs about what's possible keep you playing small; and if uncertainty about how to get things right stop you from even starting, then the world will be robbed of the huge value you and your ideas represent.

MANAGING SELF-DOUBT

Doubt, fear and uncertainty are all common feelings. They will accompany you through every stage of the next chapter change cycle—this is completely normal and to be expected. The challenge is to ensure these emotions don't stop the process of change and expansion, smothering your desires, creating lengthy detours, or even derailing your vision altogether. The solution to staying out of this stagnation cycle is to be aware of your old stories, to feel doubt, experience fear and face uncertainty, and continue to move forward regardless.

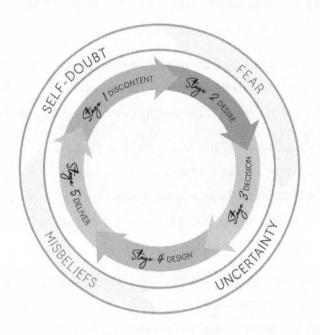

The Stagnation Cycle

I wholeheartedly believe that your level of self-worth has a direct effect on what's possible for you in the future. Without a strong connection to your innate worthiness you will find it difficult to act on your desires, value your contributions, give yourself permission to choose the work that most fulfils you, and allow yourself to receive the financial rewards available to you. With a strong connection to your self-worth, you can access confidence, creativity, courage and resilience, plus many more incredibly empowering and energising emotions.

Doubt and fear can create misbeliefs that prevent you reaching the potential that you know is inside of you. They are simply habits, strong feelings created by your thoughts that you've heard so often you've come to believe them. But because you have agency over your thoughts, because they are within your control, you can change them; you can adjust your relationship with these constricting emotions and reconnect to your power.

You can learn how to change self-sabotage, procrastination, comparison, perfectionism—all the things that may have held you back until now and stopped you stepping into your next chapter. You can make friends with these emotions; you can recognise and even welcome them because of the lessons they have for you. You can choose to change the story you've created around them, which are simply misbeliefs, and begin a whole new narrative that puts you in the driver's seat, taking consistent, confident action on your ideas.

Doubt and fear will no longer be able to dictate your actions and reactions, even if they are still in the room with you—as they probably will be.

Doubt and fear are part of who we are. They're evolutionary markers, hangovers from prehistoric times when we faced constant physical dangers. The amygdala—the almond-shaped section of nervous tissue located in the temporal lobe of the brain—is part of the limbic system, which is responsible for our emotions and survival instincts; it is the origin of the fight, flight or freeze reaction to threats. Prehistorically, it made sense to assume the rustle in the bushes was something likely to eat us rather than just a gentle, cooling breeze, because there was a high likelihood that it was.

Today, this natural defence mechanism continues to kick in, even though physical threats are not usually a daily occurrence. The amygdala is kept gainfully employed as our inner critic, reacting to emotional rather than physical threats, working to keep us safe when it perceives we are at risk.

Emotional threats can be many and varied, like launching a business in an area that you really care about. Introducing a new service line that takes you in a whole different direction. Publishing a blog post in which you share your opinion. Stepping onto a stage to speak. Explaining what it is you do at a networking event.

You likely already know the physical sensations. Your personal recipe will be unique to you, but it probably includes some combination of a sinking sensation in your stomach, sweaty palms, a nervous tic, a fast pulse pounding in your ears, dry mouth, closed throat, headache, nausea, racing heart, and perhaps a general, unspecified feeling of impending doom.

You may not be consciously anticipating a fear response, but your body knows. Your emotions are always felt in your body first, which is why they're called feelings.

And then the thoughts kick in:

- What are you doing?
- You're not ready for this.
- Who do you think you are?
- They're going to laugh at you.
- It'll be so obvious you don't know what you're talking about.
- Everyone here is so much more advanced than you, so just keep quiet.
- Better play it safe and take out those paragraphs.
- You don't have to record that video now; do it later.
- You're so stupid.
- How could this possibly work?
- No one will be interested.
- Of course he didn't call back; he thinks your proposal is ridiculous.
- You'll never get another client.
- Why are you surprised you didn't get the numbers you expected?
- You'll never be as good as her so why even bother trying?

These fiercely critical thoughts are the birthplace of doubt and the crematorium of dreams. They can create pessimism, disillusionment, overwhelm and anxiety, rolling them all up into a story of what is not possible for you. And none of these feelings, or any of their emotional cousins, is likely to facilitate inspired action.

It's not who you are that stops you from expanding; it's who you think you're *not*. It's a common narrative that your inner critic feeds you in a misguided effort to keep you safe.

Another side to this fear and inadequacy landscape that keeps us quiet and invisible needs to be discussed as well: we can be constricted by the fear of being seen as arrogant. In my hometown it was referred to as 'being too big for your boots'. In Australia we call it the 'tall-poppy syndrome'.

There is a tendency in both countries to mock those who have the audacity to think highly of themselves, to display confidence in their views and abilities. It's a ploy that is often presented playfully, rather than in the unfortunately fierce way I experienced as a young teen, but ultimately it's harmful because it often leads to self-deprecation and the avoidance of any kind of spotlight.

Your inner critic will latch onto these comments and feelings, and replay them when you're feeling vulnerable.

If you have the misfortune to experience this phenomenon, as I did as a teen, take a moment to remind yourself that you don't need to take on other people's opinions. I like to imagine myself wrapping those miraculous gold bands that Lynda Carter wore as Wonder Woman around my wrists, and having hurtful observations, or even just the memory of them, bounce harmlessly off my bracelets. Pow! Pow!

YOUR RESOURCEFUL INNER CRITIC

What a delightful arsenal of weaponry your inner critic has to use against you. She knows you and your tender spots so well. The dialogue running through your head is most often what leads you to playing small, or maybe not even playing at all. Your inner critic's messages are the barriers to you fully embodying your potential and reaching your next chapter. It's not your actual lack of experience, skill, luck, talent or clarity: it is your inner critic's messages.

Your inner critic uses emotional tricks to keep you contained and to discourage you from expanding fully into what you desire. Sometimes she will even prevent you from seeing or defining what that desire is for you. She is opinionated, hypercritical, relentless, repetitive, and determined to show you all the ways in which you are not enough.

If you could see your critic standing in front of you right now, she would likely have her arms folded and a look of disdain on her face. As far as she's concerned, her job is to keep you safe, and the most effective strategy she has is to remind you of all the ways in which you don't measure up.

I have affectionately named my own inner critic Helga, more specifically, Horrible Helga in High Heels. I even found a photo online that depicts Helga exactly as I imagine her.

I see her sitting in a corner happily knitting. She's completely relaxed and seemingly disinterested in me as long as I stay within my comfort realm, my area of familiarity, and don't take any chances. The moment she senses me approaching a growth edge, stepping into something new that could involve risk or the possibility of being judged, entering a situation where I don't have all the answers, she tosses her knitting aside and races to the centre of the room. She starts wagging her finger at me and tells me, always insistently and often quite aggressively, all the ways in which I will fail.

Another of her strategies is to allow me to feel excited and buoyant about a new idea, uplifted with positivity for a few days … and then to show up, quietly pouring cold water on my initial clarity and enthusiasm. I've seen this play out with women I've taken on retreat or worked with in

VIP planning days so often that I've termed the experience the Kerdonk Factor. I pre-warn them to be prepared for this emotional hijacking and influx of doubt, and to not allow it to take them off course or make them believe that their newly laid plans should be abandoned.

I've yet to meet a woman without this negative self-talk going on inside despite how calm, successful and together they appear on the outside. Women are, almost without exception, hard on themselves. Generally speaking, women put themselves way down the priority totem pole. We are more likely to criticise and berate ourselves when we don't meet our own expectations than we are to acknowledge and celebrate ourselves when we do. We would never pour doubt on others the way we do on ourselves.

Fortunately, I've dealt with a deluge of doubt and fear over the years and have become familiar with Helga's tricks. I know that the best way to navigate the road ahead is to make peace with her, not to fight or ignore her.

I have discovered simple and effective practices that help other women deal with their own inner critic and the accompanying doubt, fear, pain, uncertainty, anxiety and other members of this emotional family. I have taught these practices and tools to a great many of my clients as they step bravely into the next version of themselves and I'm sure you'll find them equally useful as you discover them in this book.

As psychologist and author Susan Jeffers says, 'Feel the fear and do it anyway.'[11] This will allow you to focus on expanding your capacity for self-trust. If what you desire is real, deep and destined for you, then doubt is inevitable. If your desires weren't important, you wouldn't feel bothered. So I encourage you to welcome doubt, fear and uncertainty as evidence of how important your next chapter is, and to work on developing the self-awareness, self-compassion and self-belief that will allow you to manage these emotions deftly.

THE SELF-WORTH TRILOGY

What tools of equal strength and power can you access to make peace with your inner critic, persuade her to lay down her verbal sword and step aside? There are three powerful pieces in this peace pact that I've combined into a philosophy that I call the 'self-worth trilogy'. Since each stage has exercises and practices for you to complete, it's a good time to have your journal beside you.

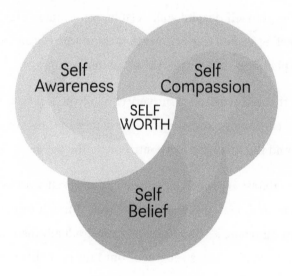

The Self-Worth Trilogy

In the past, I thought confidence was the key to a successful next-chapter venture. I've since come to realise that although confidence is important, it is usually related to your perceived competence in a specific area, which means it can fluctuate. You can be confident about your cooking skills, but unsure about your ability to play a sport. You can be confident about your ability to write a blog post, but not about how you'll handle the reactions to that post.

Your confidence does increase as your experience and competence grow, and your self-esteem expands right alongside. But as both confidence and self-esteem are significantly determined by external factors that you ultimately cannot control, relying on them alone to help you navigate doubt and fully express your desires can be a little perilous.

You need to focus on and cultivate a deeper, more anchored and enduring sense of self. Self-worth is that deeper sense. Self-worth is a measure of how you view yourself despite your results, what others may think, or what's happening around you. Self-worth is about who you are, the unique qualities, experiences and perspectives that make you, you.

This means that self-worth is at the very core of you. It is your thoughts, feelings, and behaviours woven together to determine how you view your worthiness and the value you can contribute to the world.

Your goal, therefore, is to anchor yourself in strong self-worth so you can truly blossom. Although this state is first built through feedback about your accomplishments, it's important that you gradually disconnect from this external validation and strengthen your internal belief in yourself.

Your personal vision is built around the contribution you want to make in the world. It's your lighthouse, and self-worth is your anchor, holding you firm even when challenges and doubts buffet you.

The self-worth trilogy supports this vital move away from relying primarily on external feedback and towards trusting yourself. I have a core message on my website that encapsulates this transfer of trust: *Borrow my belief in you until you have it for yourself.* This message reflects what I have come to know:

- First, you need someone else to believe in you, in your ideas and your potential.
- Second, you begin to believe in that person and their faith in you.
- Third, you move to full reconnection with your own worthiness and develop a strong sense of self-belief in your ability to contribute in a unique way.

Most importantly, it's about getting to a place where you no longer wonder if you are valuable; rather, you simply ponder and explore *how* you will express that value.

One of the fabulous truths about ageing is that the need for approval tends to decrease, and as this change is a fundamental piece in the foundation of your self-worth, the shift to appreciating your inherent value can be swift when you have awareness, and some key tools and exercises. The door to your next chapter can swing open freely on newly lubricated hinges.

Working with the self-worth trilogy involves cultivating the three key qualities that underpin healthy, enduring self-worth:

1. Self-awareness
2. Self-compassion
3. Self-belief

1. Harness the power of self-awareness

Psychologist Daniel Goleman, author of *Emotional Intelligence*,[12] defines self-awareness as 'knowing one's internal states, preferences, resources, and intuitions, as well as their effect on others', a definition I like as it emphasises the importance of monitoring our inner world, our thoughts and emotions.

Your ability to consciously choose thoughts that support you taking action on your next-chapter desires and goals is an important skill to develop. You will find it helpful to identify your inner critic as a part of this process, to increase your awareness of her presence so you can externalise, personify and recognise what she says and when. This familiarity decreases her power and impact.

Your inner critic most often makes an appearance when you're on a growth edge, when you're stepping outside of your familiarity realm, stretching, trying something new. That is when you're most likely to meet her.

These are universal experiences. When you recognise your critic's voice and messages, it gives you the space and grace to respond, rather than react. You can stage an intervention on yourself, asking why you're having that particular thought. Then you can consciously choose a different one that shepherds you away from a debilitating emotional landscape peppered with bogs of doubt, fear, misbeliefs, procrastination, comparison and inaction.

As we all do, you have a core critic: the judge. The judge leads the critic team, judging you, judging others, and judging your environment and experiences with automatic reactions, holding them up against what she believes to be right, true and proper, and then giving her verdict. That verdict is usually black or white, good or bad, acceptable or lacking, with very little wriggle room.

When you can intercept these judgments and let them go it will allow space for pure observation, a space where you can notice, learn and potentially grow. It takes practice to notice when you are judging someone or something, then interrupt this habit of a lifetime. It also takes emotional dexterity and self-compassion to avoid judging yourself for judging. But I urge you to persevere because the benefits are significant: a feeling of peace and calm, an expansion of acceptance, a lessening of the need to compete, a heightened appreciation for diversity, an increase in inspiration and creativity, and a deepening of your own capacity for delight.

Accompanying your core critic—the judge—are your critics in command. There are typically five common roles adopted by critics in command, all with corresponding conditions for worthiness: the comparison queen, the people pleaser, the perfectionist, the overachiever, and the imposter.

The comparison queen

This critic demands that you be better than other people to be worthy, and this means she can rain on your parade very quickly. She's my own critic in command and I'm intimately acquainted with her language and tools of deflation.

Even when you have created something special that you feel pride in—a piece of art, a new business offering, a gorgeous new outfit, a new idea—your comparison queen will pop up and flaunt someone else's work in your face and then taunt you. *Yes, not too bad I suppose, but have you seen this?*

She likes to remind you of how ridiculous and unlikely your desires are, or how you really don't measure up in very specific areas of your life compared to how well other people are doing. Her constant reminders of this are likely to make you feel inferior, and you will doubt your ideas and your ability. When she gets started, you can find yourself spiralling down a rabbit hole pretty quickly, feeling that you're way behind the eight ball and will never catch up to those who have already 'made it'.

The comparison queen is a major driver of self-sabotage.

> *Sharleen:* 'Oh, I know my comparison queen really well. She pops up all the time. I was always jealous of my older sister and constantly compared myself to her, so that was the likely starting point for my comparison queen's observations: *You're not smart enough. You don't know enough. Who's going to listen to you? Not another course in this; so many others are offering this topic and doing it better. She's more popular than you, look how many people she has in her community. She must be good because she has lots of money and you're still striving for financial freedom.*'

The people pleaser

This critic demands that you become whoever others want you to be to be worthy. With this critic in charge, you're terrified that no one will like you if you don't put everyone else first and do the right, good, expected thing. She pushes you to make decisions based on how others will perceive you and how you can best please them.

She uses words like 'should' and 'must', and you're likely to find yourself with an ever-increasing array of masks to wear, depending on whom you're with and what you think will keep them happy. Consequently, your boundaries are often non-existent because she firmly believes that the most important thing is being seen as a good person doing the right thing, and keeping everyone else happy. You are definitely last on the list and her dominant message is: *You can't do that. What will they think?*

The intense need to please and care for others that this critic displays is deeply rooted in a fear of rejection. Over time, it can lead to resentment, stress and even depression.

> *Karen:* 'She shows up every time I have to make a decision that might negatively impact other people, even more so if I'm going to benefit from the decision. When she's in charge I feel the need to make sure that everyone else is looked after. She locks up my productivity with an endless ongoing dialogue in my head around me doing the right thing, especially regarding my employees, and especially the underperforming ones.'

> *Pascale:* 'Whenever I start a new job or project, she tells me I'm not good enough to do it well and wonders how on earth I landed the gig. She also makes frequent appearances when I'm in a new situation and unsure of who I'm working or dealing with.'

The perfectionist

This critic demands that you get everything right to be worthy. Mistakes cannot be tolerated. She's an expert at highlighting your shortcomings and pointing out how you don't meet her unrealistic expectations.

She is relentless in her expectations with 'go hard or go home' as her mantra. If you feel that your appearance, your home, or anything you create needs to be perfect before it can be seen, then you're at the mercy of this relentless inner critic. She's afraid that if something isn't flawless, you'll be judged, rejected, dismissed, or even ridiculed, and you feel driven to constantly improve.

She can paralyse you, either by making you work endlessly on projects that are never quite good enough, or preventing you from getting started because you fear it won't be good enough.

Because she places so much stock in results, anything less than perfection is perceived as failure. Procrastination is a common side effect when she gets hold of you. You procrastinate because you know she won't be satisfied with what you do so you can't see the point of starting. Her most common catcall: *Is that the best you can do?*

With the perfectionist holding the steering wheel, your best ideas are often left on the drawing board, never to see the light of day.

> *Jane:* 'Oh, the perfectionist, she's always with me. She thinks I could do everything better, and so things often take longer than I'd like. But I simply have to check details and facts and learn the proper way to do something as I go.'

> *Sonya:* 'My perfectionist comes out in a few different ways. I procrastinate through fear of not doing something perfectly. I spend too long on paid jobs because they have to be perfect to my eye. I always meet the deadline, but I spend more time than I've quoted for. I suspect she's also responsible for the fear of putting my writing out into the world, thinking it's not good enough. I'm working on that one right now.'

The overachiever

This critic demands that you do more, learn more, and be more to be worthy. If you feel like you have it all under control on the outside but hear a very different dialogue on the inside, this is your overachiever speaking. This is the human *doing* not the human *being* inner critic, the one who cracks the whip and always has you working on several things at once, doing everything you can to prove your value.

She loves being seen as an amazing juggler: 'I don't know how you do it' is coveted high praise to her. Her messages are shot through with a streak of martyrdom that will give you a sense of guilt, making you accept more and more responsibility.

Her motivation comes from being seen as highly dependable and capable. She is addicted to the pursuit of goals, often without questioning if she truly wants the prize or end result. If you find it difficult to relax, or feel guilty about sitting still for too long, it's highly likely that this inner critic is saying to you: *Get up and get on with it.*

This is also a common form of numbing behaviour; keeping busy, busy, busy is a highly effective way of avoiding feelings that are uncomfortable. When the overachiever is in control you can become overwhelmed, physically compromised and emotionally wrung out. You seldom pause and allow space for appreciating what you have done. You have no time for contemplation or self-care, and that makes it very difficult to hear what your heart really desires.

> *Kylie:* 'I can see how she controls me. I'm over-promising and over-de-livering to my clients. To be honest, the only person I under-deliver to is myself. She tells me that I can't say no, makes me offer to work to really short deadlines and always go beyond. She exhausts me.'
>
> *Andrea:* My critic tells me: *You get these fifteen things all done.* I end up making big plans that I can't always achieve, and then I struggle

to ask for help because her high expectations are created on the basis that I see others doing those things so I should be able to, too. She shows up regularly when I'm feeling stressed and overwhelmed, and then she exacerbates these feelings.'

The impostor

This critic demands that you prove yourself to be worthy. She has you batting away compliments and downplaying your success, dismissing it as luck, timing, or as a result of deceiving others into thinking you're more intelligent and competent than you actually are. She is both convinced that you don't deserve praise and terrified that you'll be seen as arrogant if you accept it.

The impostor undermines you by downplaying any evidence that supports your talent. She reminds you that you've only made it to this point by happenstance and you're sure to be exposed as a fake at any moment. To her, it's just a matter of time.

She's particularly noisy when you're in novel situations, like starting a new business, launching a new service, or perhaps even writing a book for the first time. These are very common situations in which you'll find this critic waiting. And there is an ironic twist to her; the more experience and expertise you do acquire, the more she makes you feel like you still have a lot to learn.

It's the imposter who prevents you from allowing yourself to be seen and taking the risks that lead to growth and fulfilment.

Jo: 'The imposter is my critic in command. She turns up the minute I'm outside my comfort zone, and the minute I'm asked a question or receive an enquiry about my business services, saying: *You can't do it. You don't know enough. Someone else can do it better. Someone else is more qualified. What if you mess up?'*

Jodi: 'I'm terrible at resisting my imposter. She makes sure I constantly defer to other people's expertise, or don't do things at all because I feel that I don't know enough.'

It's helpful to identify your critic in command, the one who accompanies the judge, and to be aware when she stands up and tries to flatten you. Awareness is power because it opens the door to action. You may also feel that some, or even all, of the other critics are familiar as well, which is highly likely because critics can show up in more than one guise, depending on the situation you find yourself in, but you're still likely to have a dominant character.

You can take the quiz on my website to discover who she is: www. angelaraspass.com/takethequiz. When you've pinned a badge on her it will be easier to recognise when she's trying to take the reins. Then you can choose to mindfully refute her outbursts and make peace with her.

My comparison queen has been a regular visitor throughout the writing of this book, forever reminding me that compared to other books I've read throughout my life, my attempt just doesn't measure up. I've thanked her and reassured her because I know she's simply trying to protect me from the judgment and possible rejection she's sure I'll experience as an actual author, rather than as a potential author. The latter may be safer, but the former, committing to becoming an actual author, is the territory of my truth and that's where I choose to live these days.

Now it's time to identify the ways in which your critic has held you back. You know that your inner critic is likely to hinder you from reaching your full potential, taking a chance, trying something new, and from claiming your true self-worth; she deters you from so many things.

Take some time to reflect on this. The following questions will help:

- What price have I paid?
- What desires have I denied?
- What dreams have I kept inside?
- Have I held myself back or stayed in my familiar realm because she's been in control?

It's time to get really clear on what it costs you to continue to allow her to run the show, keeping in mind that she may have been driving your thoughts and feelings, and therefore your responses and behaviours, for years. Once you become aware of this and have new tools to work with, you'll be inspired and empowered to change things.

Keep exploring. Perhaps she has stopped you from doing one or more of the following:

- Applying for a new role or asking for a promotion
- Taking up a new hobby
- Trying out a new sport
- Letting go of a relationship that no longer serves you
- Pursuing a relationship that you really wanted
- Setting boundaries
- Starting a business
- Creating a new product or service
- Removing a service or product that no longer resonates for you

- Increasing your rates
- Standing up for yourself
- Expressing how you really feel
- Asking for what you want
- Taking good care of your body

Spend some time here. Be honest with yourself. Then look back at your list. Is there a good reason to allow her to continue her reign?

You have literally thousands of thoughts each and every day, and you may be surprised to know that the great majority of them loop on repeat, especially when your inner critic holds the reins.

I have a wonderfully talented client who has struggled with allowing herself to be seen online. Her work is powerful and beautiful. She helps women in business create their visual brands and messaging, and market in a way that aligns with their values so they can show up confidently and authentically. It may seem somewhat ironic that her inner critic stops her from doing the very thing that she sets her own clients free to do, but it's a paradox that I've seen often.

She has a very vocal inner critic who allows her to post about her vulner-abilities online but leaps up and berates her when she considers posting a celebration or success, or an invitation for women to work with her. This voice of doubt about the likelihood of anyone responding, or the value of what she's about to share, reinforces an old sense of not being good enough. That feeling stifles her creativity, quietens her voice, drowns out inspiration and prevents her from regularly marketing herself. The inaction, a direct response to her thoughts, further reinforces her self-image of not being enough. *See, I can't even promote myself. If I can't practise what I preach, how can I possibly teach others?*

Sometimes she does manage to beat her critic to the 'post now' button, but a lack of consistent promotion becomes a self-fulfilling prophecy as her business grows in fits and starts rather than in the steady way her talent and skill deserve.

A similar type of behaviour that your own inner critic is responsible for is seldom in your best interests, but it can be changed when you focus on awareness. Begin to notice reactions, patterns or habitual responses you recognise in yourself when she is in control. Spend some time reflecting. Ask yourself if you do any of the following:

- Give up
- Push yourself down the priority totem pole
- Procrastinate
- Get angry
- Feel really anxious
- Find yourself short of breath
- Act arrogantly and belligerently
- Withdraw
- Complain about how unfair the world is
- Research more
- Gather opinions from everyone
- Reminisce about the good old days
- Distract yourself by being busy and preoccupied
- Numb yourself though eating, drinking, shopping, etc.
- Do 'the right thing' regardless of how you feel

These reactions are both common and understandable, but they won't serve you when it comes to responding to your desires and stepping into your next chapter.

Personifying and externalising your inner critic helps you to reduce her power. Find or draw a picture of your inner critic and give her a name. When you have identified her as an entity with depth and weight, rather than simply as a vague feeling, you'll find it much easier to work with her.

Become aware of how she talks to you. Recognise her patterns. What words does she use? Are there key phrases that come up again and again? Does she speak with a certain tone of voice? Don't try to fight or resist her. You may have heard the expression, 'What you resist, persists.' You can acknowledge her, but then claim your power to choose not to believe what she has to say, to not fall for the misbeliefs.

It's time to change the meaning you take from the stories she tells. To do this, start by adjusting your zoom lens. When you're feeling shame, fear or doubt and move straight into berating yourself, you have your camera lens zoomed in tight. All you can see is your flawed self, alone in your mistakes or inadequacy. You may believe you're the only one in this situation; that there's something wrong with you and you are alone and wanting.

But when you zoom out, when you hear stories from other women who are also facing and dealing with a regular barrage of critical thoughts, you gain a completely different perspective. You can see that what you're experiencing, thinking and feeling is far more universal than you could have imagined. Revisit those story snippets that the women who answered my survey shared. Are they similar to the stories your critic tells you?

With practice, you will begin to notice when it's your critic talking, and that self-awareness will allow you the space to recognise and respond, rather than accept and acquiesce.

As Victor Frankel said, 'Between stimulus and response there is a space. In that space is our power to choose our response. In our response lies our growth and our freedom.'

Your freedom is waiting for you, too.

2. Create a self-compassion plan

The next stage in the self-worth trilogy, as you move towards making peace with your inner critic and step forward into Your Next Chapter, is developing self-compassion. Self-contempt is fuel for her, and when you remove that fuel source, replacing it with self-compassion, kindness and understanding, she runs out of steam.

This is all about softening your inner dialogue, especially now that you're building the skill of self-awareness that allows you to recognise the berating, non-supportive tone as belonging to your inner critic.

These days I have an unconditional friendship with myself. I know I have my own back. I offer myself a safe place to land when I'm disappointed or afraid, and I speak to myself in an encouraging, kind and supportive tone. Sometimes I simply laugh at what Helga tries to convince me of. It's taken me a while to make it to this place. My natural state used to be to treat myself extremely harshly.

Before sobriety—before I learned that I was not a bad person who needed to become good, but rather a person who needed to become well—I regarded myself with a mixture of disgust and mistrust, and my internal dialogue was cruel and derogatory. That approach trapped me in a cycle of despair and addiction. I now know that no one can improve and grow when they are beating themselves up or putting themselves down.

Today, thanks to radically improved self-awareness and self-compassion, I ensure that I speak to myself very differently. Helga has largely retreated, sat down and returned to her knitting.

This shift is of course, a practice. The more often you turn to self-compassion when your inner critic arrives, the easier it will be to turn down the volume on her nasty edge and replace it with soothing thoughts and words. You'll be on your way to escaping her clutches.

I highly recommend developing a self-compassion plan so you're ready when life throws you a curve ball, or when your judge and your critic in command become difficult to ignore and those moments of self-doubt hit.

When you face challenges, when you're feeling disappointed or when things haven't gone quite how you would have liked them to, will you take care of yourself with the same loving kindness that you would offer a good friend in the same situation? When you're upset, hurt or disappointed, acknowledge it. Don't try to fight the reality of how you're feeling. Console yourself with kindness and then move into positive, reassuring action.

Take proactive action by building a self-compassion plan that works for you. What is deeply reassuring or even just pleasantly distracting? How will *you* take care of *you*?

When building your self-compassion plan, it's important that you distinguish between what is genuinely nourishing and supportive—a hot bath, a walk in nature or a call to a good friend—and what is a numbing behaviour, something that alleviates the original pain but by its very nature creates a secondary pain. Food, alcohol, drugs, these are obvious examples of numbing behaviours, but I've also heard women hiding behind things like picking fights with loved ones, shopping for things they can't afford or don't really need, or diving headfirst into social media for hours.

There are myriad ways you can attempt to provide yourself with cold comfort, so how do you tell the difference between what is helpful and what is harmful? In my experience, when it's not a genuine act of self-compassion, there is a sense of rebellion or defiance associated with the action, a feeling of *I'll show you* or an *I don't care if it's not good for me, I want it and I deserve it* thought. You defy anyone to challenge your right to the behaviour.

I know this response intimately because I used to 'get drunk at the world' with what I saw as justified anger and indignation, and it never, ever helped. In direct contrast, when I replaced false pleasures with genuine, compassionate and joyful care, my life improved and my connection to my self-worth strengthened. For me, this included simple things like investing in essential oils and candles, developing a meditation and journaling practice, using the power of music to quickly change my mood, and learning to reach out for help.

So please don't wait until life gives you a kick in the pants and you have to react. With a little thoughtful forward planning you'll be able to respond with kindness and bounce back a little easier.

Take the time to develop a personal self-compassion plan. Capture your initial ideas in your journal and leave space to add to them as new thoughts arise. This is another situation where your expanded emotional vocabulary will prove its value. Following are some suggestions for a self-compassion plan:

When my inner critic arrives and I'm feeling vulnerable ...

- I will pause and breathe deeply, at least three to five times.
- I will deliberately tense my entire body and then relax and experience the contrast.
- I won't fight what I'm feeling or try to push it away. I'll acknowledge what I'm experiencing and articulate it: *This feels hard. This feels painful. This feels scary. This is how I feel.*
- I'll stop myself from past pondering or future tripping.
- I won't catastrophise or get stuck in the story.
- I'll connect to the present by focusing on what I can see, hear and feel around me.

And then I will find alternative ways of dealing with my feelings ...

- Light a candle
- Take a bath
- Meditate
- Spend some time with my pet
- Read inspirational quotes
- Play my favourite music and dance it off
- Get outside into nature
- Make a cup of my favourite tea
- Reach out/connect with a belief buddy (a trusted ally who knows about and supports my Next Chapter Vision, however hazy it may initially be)
- Dive into my fabulous file (see the next section for details)

3. Build self-belief with a fabulous file

Self-belief is the third component of the self-worth trilogy. It means having trust in your ideas, abilities and judgment. The core word in this definition is *trust*. The beautiful thing is that self-trust increases as we age, as we begin to detach more from the opinions of others and rely more on our own inner knowing.

Self-knowledge builds trust. Seeing and internalising the fact that you can do things you set your mind to builds trust. Noticing that you can add value to the world by helping others builds trust. Valuing your unique contribution builds trust.

Self-belief is transferable. So even if you've never done something before, like starting a business, the fact that you've put your mind to other endeavours and succeeded throughout your life will help build your self-belief, when you allow it to.

Knowing that you matter to people in your life is another self-belief building block, as is acting in alignment with your values.

The key is to acknowledge these events and facts and ways of being, and one of the best ways of doing this is by creating and regularly visiting what I call a 'fabulous file'.

A fabulous file is a physical file that holds examples, big and small, of your fabulosity: client feedback, goals achieved, screenshots of comments and feedback on social media, cards received, photographs at events, and goals you've hit. Anything that makes you smile and feel good about what you've experienced, contributed and achieved.

It's essential that your fabulous file is physical, not digital. Just as putting pen to paper engages your brain and emotions in ways significantly different from fingers to keyboard, the ritual of printing out and storing these shining snippets of your life engages your emotions, connects you to your abilities, and anchors your sense of impact. As you gather the contents of your fabulous file, your self-belief builds right alongside it.

I've kept my file for over eight years now and it's something I encourage all of my clients to create as well. We all go through ups and downs with our confidence and self-belief, and my fabulous file has proven to be a very handy tool for making peace with my inner critic during those low moments.

Stepping into your next chapter brings with it inevitable steep learning curves and this might have you focusing on how far you have to go to achieve all of your goals, rather than looking back and appreciating how far you've come. But when you do pause and reflect on your progress in a process I call reverse-gapping, you will find it provides *future fuel*: the burst of energy, resilience and inspiration that allows you to continue taking the consistent action that keeps you moving towards your vision.

A fabulous file, a dossier of your capabilities, helps to remind your inner critic that you're fully capable of growth. So, gather your evidence and get started. The process in and of itself is inspiring and uplifting.

Print out feedback and emails. Pull the cards and photos out of the drawer. Blow the dust off your certificates. Collect it all and keep it in the one spot.

What can you include? Here are some examples from my own fabulous file:

- Cards from my kids telling me I'm a great mum

- Photos of holidays with friends
- Boarding passes from overseas trips to conferences for my business
- An awards-night program from the network I used to run
- Photos from retreats
- Thank-you cards from clients
- Photos of flowers I've been sent
- Screenshots of social-media comments
- Printed-out emails of thanks and appreciation
- Messages from LinkedIn connection requests
- Photos from Next Chapter dinners I've hosted
- Podcast reviews
- Screenshots of my growing newsletter subscribers
- Photo of the home page of my new website
- Screenshots of my bank account when the funds arrived from a big project

At first my fabulous file was in a manila folder. Now it fills a great big box to the brim and whenever Helga tries to discourage me from stepping onto a new growth edge, whenever I'm feeling doubt, whenever I need to remind myself why I do what I do, I roll around in my fabulous file for a while and reconnect to my self-belief. Invariably it makes me feel a whole lot better, and I can exhale, square my shoulders and take the next step towards my vision. It works a treat, and not just for me.

Danielle: 'In 2015, I created my fabulous file by decorating a simple black gift box and turning it into a beautiful affirmations keepsake. The box held newspaper and magazine clippings, various articles, social-media messages, and emails about my book *Sleepy Magic*. The file was a powerful and positive tool that helped me push through moments of self-doubt and kept me motivated to reach my goals.'

Get started on your own fabulous file with these four steps:

1. Set aside some time. I guarantee you will find yourself disappearing down a rabbit hole of memory gazing in a good way.

2. Purchase a box that delights you. Consider decorating it if you're creatively minded like Danielle.

3. Don't restrict yourself to testimonials. Remember, good feelings are transferable. Where else have you been fabulous in life? Where have you been brave? Where have you stepped out of your comfort zone? Where have you stepped up and reached a goal or done something you dreamed about?

4. Keep your fabulous file nearby. Add to it regularly and visit it often to anchor yourself in the awareness of your fabulosity.

Self-awareness, self-compassion and self-belief, the three components of the self-worth trilogy, are foundational. Each builds on the others and together they help you to gradually create and reinforce an enduring connection to your worth. This makes it possible for you to step forward into the unknown, to trust yourself to take a chance and expand into the next chapters of your business and life.

THE CATCH-AND-DETACH PROCESS

The final tool I recommend to help you navigate through uncertainty is a process that you can rely on in a moment of doubt or fear. Knowing you have a reliable, immediate and tangible way to respond when your emotions are running amok is invaluable. I call this the catch-and-detach process.

Its use assumes familiarity with your inner critic, an understanding of your vulnerability triggers, and a commitment to keep your self-awareness switched on.

This approach incorporates the components of the self-worth trilogy and utilises aspects of acceptance commitment therapy (ACT). Steven C Hayes, a psychology professor at the University of Nevada, developed ACT in 1986, based on his understanding of how language and thoughts influence our internal experiences.[13]

After training in the practice with Russ Harris in 2016, I've continued to appreciate its effectiveness when I stay connected to self-awareness.

Here's how the catch-and-detach process works:

1. Catch: Notice when tension appears; tune into your body barometer. What sensations are appearing in your body? Then notice the negative thoughts that begin to flood your mind and give them a name, as if they were a story. *Ah, here's the old story telling me I've left it too late.* Or, *Yep, there's the old story telling me I've got nothing original to share.*

2. Detach: The awareness within the catch stage gives you the vital space to pause and detach, to stop yourself fusing with your thoughts. The grace of this space allows you to identify the feelings that the story provokes (discouragement, pessimism, self-criticism, disheartenment, etc) and choose not to get caught up in the memories they're associated with.

Once you've caught the thoughts and detached from them, you can consciously reframe your thoughts and replace the old story with different, more supportive and expansive thoughts. This practice helps you to gradually dismantle the ingrained habit of believing your automatic negative thoughts and instead build a new habit of reminding yourself of your worth. You might also like to deliberately tense up your entire body, exaggerate the tension, and then let all of your muscles relax with a deep, slow exhale. I've found this helps if the thoughts and feelings that are coming up are particularly intense and threatening to hijack me.

The two steps are often enough to break the pattern and pull you out of an unworthiness spiral, but sometimes you need a little more. That's when you can refer to your self-compassion plan and choose one of the actions or activities that you've already identified as helpful and nourishing, and use them as your step three.

I use the catch-and-detach process often. I recently spent time researching the page layouts in the books of some of my favourite authors. I began to read a few sentences in one of these books, the door of doubt opened just a crack, and boom! Helga slammed down her knitting, marched right up to me, stuck her face in front of mine and started one of her familiar tirades. *Did you notice how brilliant this book is? How well-written it is? How pathetic your attempt is in comparison? How could you ever think ... ?*

Before she could build herself up to a fever pitch, I managed to catch her. I quickly put the book down as I recognised the trigger, and I named the story I was experiencing, which was the classic 'Never as good as ...'. With a few deep breaths, I connected with a sense of amusement at how vigilant Helga is around my writing, and I managed to detach myself from what could have become a nasty spiral down into criticism and procrastination. I then got in touch with a trusted friend and shared the experience with her, which meant I could shake off any remaining shadows of doubt.

At first, it can almost feel as though you need a machete to cut a new thinking trail through the undergrowth of your doubts and automatic thoughts. You might find yourself falling down into a bit of a pit a few times before you manage to notice and name what's happening for you. But with practice you'll develop a new path that's far easier to walk along, free of the weeds that used to wrap around your ankles and pull you down into doubt.

Each time you use the catch-and-detach process successfully, take a moment to congratulate yourself on loosening the hold of your critic just a little bit more.

Old stories and the misbeliefs they create can produce difficulties, detours and even derailments, and keep you stuck, off track and far from the next chapter that's waiting for you—but only if you don't commit to building your self-awareness.

And you have, or you would not be reading this book.

Couple that growing awareness with a pledge to using the tools I've outlined in this chapter. Develop a friendly, supportive and unconditional relationship with yourself. Decide, on a daily basis, to allow your desire to pursue meaningful and purposeful work to be fully expressed, and you will soon be well on your way to an exhilarating and fulfilling new chapter.

There's just that tricky little next step to negotiate now. A decision.

PART TWO

MOVING FROM DREAMING TO DOING

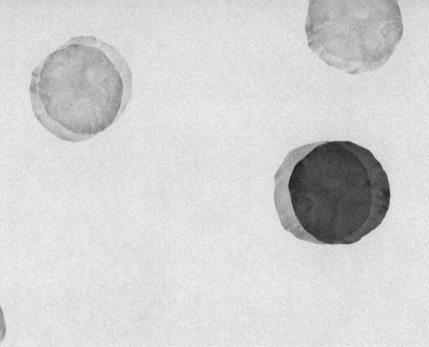

'When faced with a decision, choose the path that feeds your soul.'

Dorothy Mendoza Row

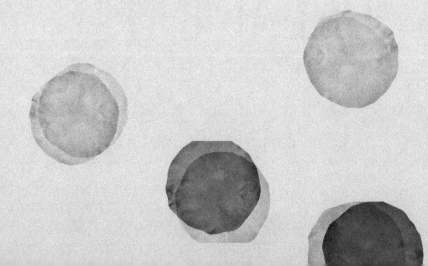

CHAPTER 4

DECISION

The Freedom to Choose

The package was delivered to my office on a Wednesday afternoon. The beautiful handwriting on the plain brown paper in the pile of mail grabbed my attention and so it was the first I opened. Inside was a set of three aromatic mists with the labels Clarity, Highest Potential and Present Moment. I spritzed one into the air and inhaled deeply, delighting in the scent. Puzzled, wondering where they had come from, I looked back into the packaging and found a card. As I read it, my heart almost leapt out of my chest:

I was in the audience when you spoke at school last year, when you encouraged us to go after our dreams, to make the decision to do the thing we've often thought about. So I did, and these mists are the result. I'd been thinking about creating them for so long, and you inspired me to take action, thank you so much. Karen.

I sat back into my chair with utter joy dancing around inside of me. I remembered that day I had spoken to the women at that Sydney school not long after I'd closed my agency and begun to do the work in the world I felt aligned with. I'd called my presentation 'Creating a Wholehearted Life', inspired by Brené Brown. It was the first time I'd given a presentation on anything other than marketing, and as I prepared, I found myself battling oscillating feelings of trepidation and excitement.

The imposter critic was rubbing her hands together with glee, delighting in reminding me that I had asked for this. A couple of months earlier, a friend had invited me to the school to hear a talk by a woman on the charity she had created. I was inspired by her story and decided then and there to approach the organiser about giving me the opportunity to do the same. And now, here I was.

Fortunately, I had a secret weapon to rely on to settle my nerves as I watched the crowd of women settling in. I call it GOSGOP, which stands for 'get off self and get on purpose'. The acronym reminds me that focusing on how I'm feeling in these situations is essentially an invitation for fear to come on in and set up camp.

To this day, before giving a presentation I visit the bathroom or some other spot where I can be alone with my thoughts. I breathe deeply and slowly and make a conscious decision to park my fears. I replace that self-focus with a connection to the collective energy of the people in the audience, to concentrate on serving them, to expand what is possible for them, to be useful, to add value.

In the auditorium that day, the ritual worked its magic, and once my nerves and I had reached a truce I stepped on stage and shared my thoughts.

I was flying as I left the school. Although I had no idea of the tangible impact my presentation would eventually have, I do recall how utterly delighted I felt. I actually punched the air as I drove out of the carpark because I felt so vibrantly alive, purposeful and joyful. There may even have been singing involved.

My goal was, and still is, to be a catalyst for women, a link in their chain of support as they expand into new possibilities in their next chapters, and it was happening because I'd made the decision to take a chance and follow my heart, just as Karen had.

A decision has energy. It's a force that sets dreams in motion. It has weight and mass and propels you down a path. It makes you square your shoulders, look uncertainty in the eye and say: *I may not have all the answers, but I'm more likely to find them when I'm in motion.*

When your desire has been shaped and focused, it's time to act. Your most compelling desires, your most fledging or fully formed and fabulous ideas that play out in the theatre of your mind, need permission to take flight in the world. And you have the power to open the door for them because everything that exists in the world first existed in someone's imagination.

THE COST OF INDECISION

The original definition of decision is from the Latin *decisionem* and means to 'to decide, determine', literally 'to cut off'. Essentially, making a decision means that a path is chosen, and other options are put to one side for now, and that reality can be terrifying and exhilarating in equal parts.

Indecisiveness is the inability to let go of alternatives when there's no hard proof that a particular way is *the* way. That's when procrastination can kick in and leave you floundering, often for a rather long time. Indecision pushes your discarded dreams under the bed and leaves them to gather dust, never having the opportunity to shine.

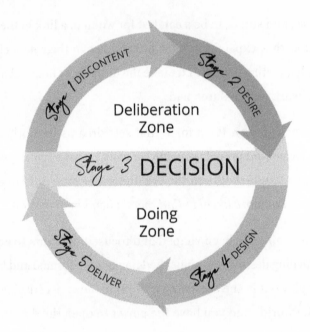

The Decision: From Deliberation to Doing

This is why the first two stages of the Your Next Chapter model of change—discontent and desire—sit in what I call the 'deliberation zone'. You can find yourself oscillating back and forth between discontent and desire, taking no action and making no progress because you haven't yet made a decision. When you get stuck here, in limbo, your dissatisfaction grows and cascades into so many other areas of your life. When you leave your dreams on the shelf, even when it seems to be your choice to do so, frustration and disappointment fester and show up in several ways.

Your lack of decision can flatten you. An open loop, a situation where uncertainty forces your mind to return to it and worry again and again, drains you of energy and enthusiasm, leaving you distracted, resigned and powerless. It's the *there's-no-point* feeling, the *I-can't-seem-to-get-out-of-bed* feeling. You move through your days in a fog, finding it difficult to motivate yourself to do much of anything. Lethargy and sadness are the typical prevailing sensations.

This sense of being stuck can also allow the discontent to deepen and taint all of your experiences. Even when you're feeling happy and content in other areas of your life, it eventually reasserts itself, jumping up from the back seat, waving its anger and disappointment in your face.

Irritability and restlessness are the emotions that take centre stage in your life. You find yourself snapping at people for no obvious reason. But you know the reason. It will continue to nibble away at the edges of your life, not allowing you to relax.

And finally, when your desires are not met with expansion and action, when your natural process of growth is thwarted, the feeling of being stuck can go a little crazy, spin out of control, painting increasingly lofty scenarios in the sky, enlarging possibilities in a desperate attempt to goad you into action. That's when your ambitions and ideas begin to seem ridiculous and unlikely, your thoughts sag into negativity, and you become vulnerable to deep doubt. *How did I ever think it was possible?* becomes your refrain, and being stuck can go from being a temporary blip to something more permanent.

The cost, when you really think about it, is high, and so the value of a decision is irrefutable. In the same way that action is the antidote to fear, understanding how to make decisions is a valuable skill to develop. You can sit and think and plan and consider your options ad infinitum, but it's only when you take action that you can test your theories, gain momentum and make the mistakes that learning curves are made of.

EVALUATING OPTIONS AND TAKING BABY STEPS

Making a decision can be a slow and tortuous process, or it can feel light as air, with you running eagerly into its outstretched arms in delight. So many factors come into play, a key piece of which is your desire for crystal-ball certainty.

Humans thrive on certainty. As much as we might like to tell ourselves that spontaneity is our desired state, we nevertheless crave anchors, and a clear direction and result when it comes to the big decisions in life.

Too many options, and the lack of a definitive outcome, can be disconcerting. You can tie yourself in knots trying to imagine and plan for a whole host of possibilities, but planning cannot equal actuality. Projection can't properly prepare you for reality and all its marvellous twists and turns. You can only partially prepare for the what-ifs, because projecting your mind forward can leave your true emotions behind. And this is why your decision needs to be anchored in desire.

Passion and commitment to a cause greater than themselves have kept humans moving forwards, eyes on the horizon, in the darkest and most challenging times.

I'm not suggesting that you throw caution completely to the wind. There are practicalities to consider. Your flights of fancy may require a reality check to ensure they're grounded in probability. You might need to focus on developing specific skills before jumping in the plane and taking the controls—if your dream is to be a pilot in your next chapter. But your dreams can reveal wings you never knew you had.

You can prepare to a point, and then faith and trust must come into play, along with acceptance. Accept that, even if things don't play out exactly as you envisage or hope, you'll be able to respond in the moment because of your strong connection to your worth.

The truth is you are already an active, experienced and accomplished decision maker. You make literally hundreds of decisions every single day but you're not aware of them because the majority are not that important and don't cause significant consequences in the great big picture of your life.

If you had to carefully weigh the pros and cons of every individual decision you make each day, your brain might explode:

- What will I have for breakfast today?
- What will I wear today?
- Should I take the dog for a walk this morning or later in the day?
- Should I open the blinds or keep them closed?
- Shall I make the bed today?
- Where will I put my keys when I come in the door?
- What brand of toothpaste will I buy this week?

Thank goodness your beautiful brain creates shortcuts, without your conscious awareness, to conserve energy and avoid decision fatigue.

You've developed these mental habits to help you more easily process the mountains of information that would otherwise smother you every day.

Habits aside, there are still a great many decisions in your life that deserve a higher level of your attention and conscious awareness. The decisions involved in starting your next chapter fall into this category, so you need to find the fertile soil between paralysis-by-analysis and impulsiveness.

I'm a proponent of the baby-steps approach. This involves taking small, consistent moves in the direction of your desire. Make bite-sized decisions. Try your desire on for size to see if it really is a good fit for you. Test things out. Take a step and see how it feels, see what eventuates. And then take the next step that reveals itself. Allow yourself to realise.

A decision is just a key to a door. It's not permanent. It's not irreversible. It's not tying you to a course of action that, once set in motion, can never be changed. A decision is simply the fuel that ignites your idea and allows it to develop. It's the first wee domino in your path that, once gently tapped, puts you into energetic motion.

How might this look in practical terms?

Maybe you've been thinking about becoming a life coach. If so, buy a book. Take a short course. Ask someone who is currently a life coach about their experiences. Speak to someone who has hired a life coach and ask them to share what their experience entailed.

If you're interested in bringing Reiki into your massage therapy, attend a presentation on the practice. Search online for information. Find out about programs running at your local college. Book yourself in for a Reiki session.

If you want to run a retreat in your business, explore venues. Spend an afternoon playing with program agendas. Connect with some of your clients and discuss your ideas. Write a page for your website. Set a date and begin.

If you've always wanted to explore photography, enrol in a low-cost online course. Lean in; get involved to see how it feels. As a good friend of mine once asked, 'Does it feel like your soul is wagging its tail?' If you can answer yes to this question, then do more of whatever it is you're doing.

The baby-steps approach allows you to explore without a deep, heavy commitment: it's simply making a decision to begin. And that decision, when given its head, can lead to unexpected, significant momentum. It can also show you that you don't want it after all, and that's an equally valuable lesson. Either way, you can't steer a parked car. You need to be in motion to take the wheel and deliberately turn it towards your destination.

MAKING CONSCIOUS CHOICES

Back when I was beginning to realise that perhaps running my marketing agency was no longer for me, several choices were available to me to change my situation. But I was afraid. I was afraid I might make the wrong decision. I felt that, even though I was miserable, it was foolish to step away from what I'd built, to step into the unknown.

Although I'd made significant progress into the realm of self-belief and had evidence that I could create something valuable from scratch, I still suspected my achievement might be a fluke. I was also hampered by my concerns about the opinions of others. I received consistent taunts from

Helga, my lovely inner critic. *What will people think? Everyone will see you as a failure and think you couldn't take the pace.*

I wrestled with these thoughts and emotions alongside a sense of responsibility to my staff and clients for several months. To close or not to close was the topic of conversation with my husband on many evenings. I must have worn out the ears of close friends at that time, too. I was firmly stuck in the deliberation zone, oscillating between discontent and desire, and grappling with doubt.

One afternoon, while reading a Wayne Dyer book I loved, *The Shift: Ambition to Meaning,*[14] I finally felt my own corresponding shift in understanding. In the book, Dr Dyer shares the stories of three quite different people who awaken to their desire to change the ways in which they are living and working. Their narratives illustrated for me the ways in which we can all embrace a powerful shift away from the ego constructs we're taught by society—constructs that emphasise achievement and accumulation—and consciously choose to turn towards a fresh focus, a life of meaning that is focused on serving and giving back.

This was exactly the type of next chapter I had seen so many people crave, choose and commit to as they moved into their second half of life.

Finally I began to understand that I, too, was deeply mired in sticky thoughts and misbeliefs about what success was, and how a business needed to look and operate to align with the definition I'd accepted, internalised and lived out. The classic, narrow, masculine version of success that I'd been subscribing to carried distinct messages: *Bigger is better. Scale and grow. Hustle and grind. Push through. Man up. It's hard but that's the price you have to pay for success.*

My first decision had to be letting go of these misbeliefs. They weren't serving me physically or emotionally and were preventing me from making different choices. This realisation allowed me a glimpse of the new freedom that was available to me on the other side of the rather bleak and restrictive landscape I'd been navigating. I had to look inside and connect to my values and desires instead of accepting someone else's rulebook. Freedom was beckoning if I could only give myself permission to decide to do things differently.

The path to this next-chapter decision was somewhat rocky and lengthy for me, so I'd like to offer you a potential shortcut by sharing the processes that eventually helped me through.

Over time, I've identified two different ways of making conscious decisions. You might find that you can easily make your choices and decisions using the stage-one steps, or you may need to venture into stage two, depending on the complexity of the issue you're considering.

Stage 1 Questions

Have you identified a decision that's asking to be made at the moment, a decision to expand a desire you've discovered? Now is the time to pause, pick up your journal and take yourself through the following steps in stage one. I've listed the six steps and then have broken each one down for you.

1. Pause
2. Check internally
3. Recognise patterns
4. Quietly question
5. Decide and trust
6. Take action

1. *Pause*: Stop for a moment. Drop the multitasking. Allow yourself the grace of space to get quiet and present so you can identify your options. Now you're ready to move onto the next step.

2. *Check internally*: I've had to learn to resist the habit of searching externally for evidence and answers. I'm slowly developing the skill of searching inside instead. When you regularly search inside you begin to become aware of how you feel when you consider your options.

   Is there a choice that feels light, uplifting, energising? Can you see this choice coming to life and playing out in the theatre of your mind?

   Does one of your options feel heavier, as if an invisible weight has settled on your shoulders and around your heart? Is it almost impossible to see a way through? This is your body barometer speaking to you, which you can liken to your intuition.

   If you feel a sudden drop in your stomach, is that natural fear or apprehension or a deep knowing that this is not the right choice for you? A feeling of expansion and warmth flowing into your chest could be excitement or confidence making itself known. Your body always speaks to you. First you need to decipher what it's saying, and then become fluent in your own body language.

3. *Recognise patterns*: As your self-awareness builds, you will become more mindful of patterns of thinking and behaviour that you naturally fall into. An understanding of your personal inner critic helps here.

   The overachiever can be in action if you have a history of making impulsive decisions. You might mistake action for traction and then regret it later, or wish you'd taken a little more time aligning your choices with your goals and priorities. If the comparison queen likes to take the reins, you may find yourself researching and amassing so many options that you lose clarity. People pleasers often seek a compliant approach, which might mean you canvass and then choose the most comfortable and popular opinion available rather than what's best for you. The perfectionist often avoids or deflects decisions in an attempt to prevent overwhelm.

If the best choice feels that it will demand a lot of you, the imposter can encourage you to simply choose the option that seems easiest, telling you that you're not up to managing anything more challenging. Understanding and recognising the typical behaviour of your personal critic means you have the opportunity to mindfully respond, backing yourself and breaking a previously unconscious pattern.

4. *Quietly question*: The more aware you become of your automatic reactions and patterns, the more comfortable and confident you will be with quietly questioning yourself. You can make sure that you're not reacting in a conditioned way, using old modes of thinking and restricting the options available to you.

Remember that you have an inner sage who is quieter than your critics, and who gifts you with a deep sense of knowing when she is given the opportunity to be heard. Ask yourself questions: *What's the truth? What's available to me? What am I not seeing?* Listen patiently to the answers. The Rumi quotation I have on my bookcase reminds me of the value of this practice: 'The quieter I become, the more I am able to hear.'[15]

5. *Decide and trust*: Tuning inwards mindfully, consciously and deliberately strengthens your ability to make decisions and to trust yourself. Your work on developing an unconditional friendship with yourself as you reconnect to your self-worth means you'll become more willing to make choices that are not necessarily going to guarantee smooth sailing. You'll become more open to challenge and growth when you know you have your own back, that even if the choice doesn't work out as you'd hoped you won't berate, harangue or desert yourself.

6. *Take action*: You've opened the door. Step through and expand.

Quite often, when you give yourself space to retreat from the busy-ness of your life, these questions provide you with the answers you seek, and you can make a clean, clear decision. But when I was in the midst of my indecision about my agency, I'd asked myself the stage-one questions a hundred and one times, and yet I still felt confused and was no closer to a clear path forward. I needed something more.

Stage 2 The Cartesian Questions

A friend introduced me to a new, focused and specific series of questions that provided the key I needed to unlock clarity and resolve. I clearly recall the evening I sat outside my home with my journal, working through them. It took me about an hour and when I'd finished, I sat quietly reading through my answers. And the truth hit me. What had to happen was so clear, and my decision was made in that moment. I crossed the threshold.

What are these magical, decision-prompting stage-two questions? They are known as Cartesian questions, and have been redeveloped from the Cartesian coordinates, a mathematical formula accredited to the French philosopher Descartes, to help with complex decision-making.[16] Each of the four succinct questions is subtly different, inviting you to deliberately examine your situation from all sides.

Here are the questions:

1. What will happen if I do?
2. What won't happen if I do?
3. What will happen if I don't?
4. What won't happen if I don't?

If, like me, you found that your own stage-one questions were not sufficient to set you free from conditioning, fear, doubt and procrastination, settle in for the structured focus of stage two.

Write each question on a separate page in your journal, putting your potential decision in the brackets. Then consider the question and begin to write freely and quickly, without allowing yourself to judge the answers that flow from the end of your pen. Don't stop. Keep going.

How did this exercise look for me? Here are just some of my answers, which careened over many pages as my emotions were uncapped and allowed free reign:

1. What *will* happen if I *do* (close the agency)?
    *   Some people may feel I have failed.
    *   Some clients will be disappointed.
    *   Some people might judge me badly.
    *   I'll have to let go of my staff.
    *   My expenses will decrease enormously.

- I won't have to put the kids in before- and after-school care anymore.
- It will be such a relief.
- I'll have breathing space to think.
- My profitability will likely increase.
- I'll be free to explore the new ideas I have.

2. What *won't* happen if I *do* (close the agency)?

- I won't get speaking gigs about marketing.
- I won't have an impressive title.
- I won't have to accept work I don't really want.
- I won't have to commute every day.
- I won't feel so damn stressed every day.
- I won't ever be able to create this level of turnover again.

3. What *will* happen if I *don't* (close the agency)?

- I'll stay feeling like this—flat and exhausted.
- I think I might implode.
- My marriage could be in jeopardy.
- My sobriety may be threatened by the stress.
- I'm likely to fire some of the clients I have.
- The standard of work we're producing will deteriorate because of my lack of focus.
- My staff will become aware of my lack of commitment and they'll become less committed, too. They may leave.

4. What *won't* happen if I *don't* (close the agency)?

- I won't have the chance to do the work that's calling me.
- I'll never know if I could have changed.
- My ideas will stay just that, ideas.

- I won't build better relationships with my family because I don't have the time.
- I don't think I'll ever manage to stop smoking.
- I won't be able to serve the people I really feel I'm here to help.

As I read back through my lists, I flipped from deliberation to action in an instant. All that agonising fell away when I saw, on paper, the reality of what my lack of decision was costing me. It's interesting, looking back, to recognise how many of the thoughts associated with this decision were projections and speculations, misbeliefs, fears and stories, and how significantly I was influenced by other people's opinions at that stage of my life.

The truth is that we have no true insight into the thoughts of others, and if we did, we'd either be shocked or pleasantly surprised at how little time they actually invest in thinking about us.

Did I know exactly what was going to happen when I made this decision? Of course not. We never know for sure the outcome of any of our endeavours. But I could now clearly hear the wisdom and reassurance of my inner sage, and I knew I couldn't continue to dismiss what she was telling me.

BREATHING SPACE FOR GROWTH

We need to give our decisions breathing space. We can plan, devise strategies and hope, but specific results are never guaranteed. Nothing is ever guaranteed or set in stone. A phone call you receive, miss or make can change everything. A chance meeting could open a new door. A book you read could spark an idea that influences a whole new direction. The business I have today is not exactly what I imagined when I began my own next chapter.

Nothing is ever certain, and, oh, the freedom in that truth.

Yes, but ...

What if you want to decide to pursue your desire but it feels like you simply can't because of circumstances out of your control? I hear you. I'm an inspired realist, by which I mean I can be lifted into the clouds with my dreams and ideas while staying grounded in reality. Your decisions have to be made in context; they are influenced by your current situation.

I'm invested in a marriage of twenty-five years and I have a daughter still at school. If my desire told me to make the decision to travel the world as a photographer, that's one decision I would be unlikely to make in this chapter my life. I could, however, take a baby step in the direction of this desire.

I could decide to take up photography as a hobby in my own neighbourhood. I could decide to go to photographic exhibitions. I could decide to join an online community. I could decide to take myself off on a photography jaunt to Tasmania for a week or so. Desire only transmutes into resentment and sadness when it's ignored and told that its existence is not possible at all; that no decision is available.

Another reality we have to face is that of our financial commitments. I knew when I pivoted from consulting to mentoring there would likely be a revenue downturn as I re-established myself, and that it would have a financial impact on my family. I needed a bridge from where I was to where I wanted to go.

When I closed my agency, I initially returned to my original freelancing roots. I took three clients with me who I really enjoyed working with. Although creating and executing marketing plans was no longer on the top of my list of desires, it was still work that I was very capable of doing, and the revenue this work provided protected my new business venture from the dangerous weight of expectation.

I looked upon these three clients as investor clients: they were investing in me so I could build my future. This attitude removed any potential resentment I could have felt from not being fully immersed in my new work, and having the clients gave me financial breathing space.

I was in the fortunate position of recognising that the goals I had developed around my next chapter were self-imposed; no one else was waiting for me to show up and perform. I had the luxury of allowing myself to develop my new endeavour slowly and sustainably. Common advice is to 'leap and grow your wings on the way down', and although I absolutely subscribe to that in terms of trusting yourself to follow your dreams, I equally believe that you need to ensure that you have a parachute, which could simply mean having a part-time job.

In the years since then I have seen the back of many a fledgling small business break under the pressure of having to mature too quickly, of having to reach inflexible goals within unrealistic timeframes.

Sky-high expectations and the subsequent stress they create can be the quickest way to squash your creativity and stifle sales conversations with anxiety. They can force you to compromise boundaries and cut corners; to push products, services and experiences out into the market that you know are not aligned with your values. They can tempt you to adopt other people's beliefs and ideas about how you should position and present yourself, making you lose connection with who you actually are. Not surprisingly, these scenarios can create a sense of anxiety and even desperation as the pressures mount, or they can tip you into despondency and procrastination.

Your new ideas need time, space and fresh air to flourish. That's why the concept of investor clients is so important. You'll know when you've reached the point where you can choose to cut yourself free, but until then the 'reassurance insurance' allows you to let go and flow.

What if you make decisions that don't turn out well? You will. I did. I do. We all do, because we are all works in progress, and the only way we can grow is by venturing into new territory, testing out theories, trying something out of our ordinary.

The consequences of our decisions are woven into the fabric of our lives in complex ways, which means we can't always see or predict the domino effect they set in motion. I've often looked back with 'kindsight' (my word for compassionate reflection) and seen that a repercussion I originally judged as nothing but negative has, with the benefit of passing time, actually morphed into something valuable. Doors have been opened into new possibilities that I could never have deliberately chosen.

When we work out physically, when we stretch ourselves out of our comfort realm, we create mini tears in our muscles, and it's the repair process that builds our strength. In a similar way, when we stretch ourselves and experience a degree of potential pain in the form of a mistake or an outcome that is different from or less than we anticipated or were aiming for, this is our opportunity to grow, to build our resilience—as long as we come from a place of self-compassion, of course.

I've mentioned that humans have a natural negativity bias. This plays out in decision-making as well, for instance, when you project your thoughts into what-could-go-wrong territory rather than allowing yourself to ponder, for a moment, what might actually go right.

Some decisions can be heart wrenching; you may feel they'll break you. But who you become on the other side could be a woman unleashed, a woman who knows her power, a woman who trusts herself. Your decisions may not always be perfect, but they are *yours*, and there is power in that fact. You can choose again and again and again, as you continue to shape the next chapter of your life.

I recently watched a short series on Netflix called *Unorthodox*. In one of the final scenes the main character, Etsy, has a deeply emotional conversation with her estranged husband, who has travelled from New York to Berlin, where Etsy has fled to start a new life. He is intent on enticing her to come back with him. It would be easy for Etsy to make the decision to return to what she knows, far less challenging than it was to strike out alone.

But she doesn't. She chooses herself. The quiet power that emanates from her small frame as she walks down the street into the unknown is palpable. She is resolute, strong. She is creating her future by making one big decision, and the many small decisions that will follow. She doesn't know where those decisions will lead her, but she is brave enough to know it's towards the future that she wants, the future that she will build one decision at a time as she steps into her inherent self-worth.

This choice is available to you, too. You might not move to an entirely new country with your decision, but you can certainly move into the territory of your dreams, and that's a destination you deserve to reach.

It's time to leave deliberation behind and step boldly into the doing zone, where you'll begin to actively design the shape and style of your next chapter.

PART THREE

PUTTING YOUR IDEAS INTO ACTION

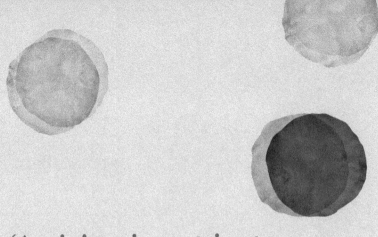

'A vision is not just a picture of what could be; it is an appeal to our better selves, a call to become something more.'

Rosabeth Moss Kanter

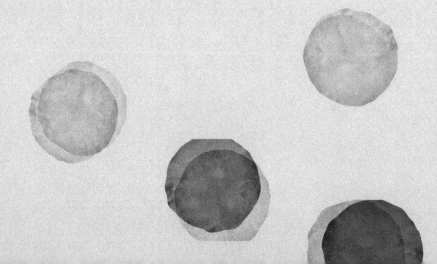

CHAPTER 5

DESIGN

Give Your Ideas Shape and Form

Grabbing my seat at the workshop on a Sunday morning, I was a little flustered. I'd travelled to the other side of Sydney, found it hard to find a carpark, even harder to find the venue, and had come close to throwing my hands up in the air and driving home. But a voice inside, my gentle inner sage, was quietly insisting that I persevere. I listen to her these days.

And so I found myself in a cosy room, sitting in a circle with about a dozen other women. As we introduced ourselves, it soon became clear to me that I was surrounded by kindred spirits. Each woman was recognising the value of her experience and feeling a strong desire to expand and contribute. In fact, I quietly pondered how every woman I'd ever worked with felt this way.

Our presenter introduced us to the concept of the soul trilogy that guides our individual journeys. It asks: What do you love to do? What do you want to create? What wants to be created through you? These were the questions she posed. I watched her draw a diagram on her flipchart and felt that familiar uplifting sensation I associate with déjà vu; it was a defining moment. I tend to think in frameworks and in visual models, and a new concept came rushing up from my heart.

A business needs to have contribution, fulfilment and financial reward in harmony for it, and its creator, to flourish.

This is a simple, powerful trilogy. The blend will look different for each of us, but it provides an overarching guide, a way of being and operating. It enriches and gives depth, meaning and personal connection to the most basic of concepts in business, which is the need to solve a problem, or address an aspiration for clients and customers.

I applied the concept retrospectively, thinking about the hundreds of business owners I'd supported and worked with since 2003, and could clearly see its resonance. The businesses that were sustainable and enjoyable had this trilogy at their core. The businesses that didn't attract customers consistently, or burnt out their owners and eventually closed, did not. My marketing agency was a prime example of the latter. A sense of contribution and financial reward were in place, but the sense of fulfilment had faded away.

If you're running a business without feeling that you're making a tangible, meaningful contribution, whatever you create and deliver will begin to feel empty and lack purpose, and over time you'll lose focus and heart.

If your work lacks a sense of personal fulfilment, a sense of deep personal satisfaction, a sense of meaning, it's equally likely that your desire to continue, especially during the more challenging times, will fade. And without claiming your value and receiving sufficient financial reward for your time, love and effort, it's likely that resentment will build, draining your energy and focus, and potentially tainting every client relationship.

All three of these components need to be in balance for your business to be emotionally and physically sustainable.

THE BUSINESS-CLARITY FULCRUM

I've shaped and shared this framework since that day. I refer to it as the 'business-clarity fulcrum' because it's vital for you to seek clear answers to these questions:

- What does contribution *mean* for you?
- What does fulfilment *feel like* for you?
- What does financial reward *look like* for you?

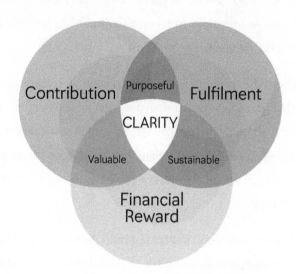

The Clarity Fulcrum

Take time to consider your responses to the three questions. Drop into your heart and ask for the answers to show themselves to you. Allow your definitions, aligned with your values and your vision, to surface. Be acutely aware of not adopting anyone else's ideas and constructs. This is your future and your story. Make space for the notion that your thoughts and ideas will change and expand over time. Next chapters are evolutions, not revolutions, and your starting point can be simple.

As I worked within this framework, something else became clear to me. The final, essential element that provides us with the clarity to define and blend these three components is self-worth. It's foundational. Emotional and physical sustainability aside, without a strong connection to our self-worth it would be a challenge for us to even begin a next-chapter business. We would find it difficult to value our contribution, hard to give ourselves permission to choose the work that most fulfils us, and almost impossible to allow ourselves to receive the financial rewards available to us for the value we create in the world.

I know we share the desire to add value, to engage in meaningful work, to feel fulfilled, perhaps even to leave a legacy. Your experiences and challenges have shaped you into the strong, smart and generous woman you are today. When you fully appreciate that, you deepen the connection to your worthiness. You are capable and valuable *because* of your experiences, not in spite of them.

The foundations of our next chapter are built on our skinned knees, our insights and lessons, and we are filled to the brim with revelations.

DESIGN PRINCIPLES

Now that you've stepped through the decision threshold and sit gazing at a blank sheet of paper that awaits your art, how do you get started on creating or recreating that blend of contribution, fulfilment and financial reward? First you go inwards, as my mentor, Michelle Richmond suggests, to connect with what you love, what you want to create, and what wants to be created through you.

Just as curiosity helped guide you to discover your desire for change, the direction and flavour of the next adventure in your life will be shaped by similar emotions that will help your work take form. Connect to those snippets of desire that have motivated, excited, energised and perhaps even outraged you; they are all unique to you. This design stage of the Your Next Chapter model of change is often the most exciting. This is when you will create a blueprint that's an incomparable expression of you, a beautiful blend of your intellect, heart and intuition. You are the emotional architect of your new world.

The combination of your intuition (your innate knowing of what's right for you that you have been honing for years), your intellect (a rich and deep reflection of your life experience), and your heart (with its focus on contribution and meaning), is formidable.

With these strengths working in unison, let's look at the components of a wholehearted framework that will guide you when you're creating a new business venture, realigning the one you already have with a new vision, or contemplating another way to contribute to the world. This could mean embracing volunteer or community work, or perhaps launching a charity or social enterprise.

Many of us start our businesses where our experience and a desire for flexibility intersect. It was my background in marketing that logically influenced my decision to begin freelance consulting. My kids were small, and I wanted the ability to fit my work around their schedules. That worked beautifully for a time, but eventually, as the demands of the business grew, I found myself reacting habitually, without pausing to consider if I actually wanted to do this work. I ended up building something that made a lot of other people happy, but often left my own desires out of the equation. The moral of this story is, of course, just because you can it doesn't mean you should.

You're looking to create something sustainable that will grow and evolve with you. You don't want this to be a shiny, fleeting idea, illuminating the world with its captivating brilliance for just a short time before fading away. To enjoy longevity, your foundations need to be strong; your sense of purpose, contribution and fulfilment need to be in alignment; and you need to be fairly compensated for the value you bring to the world.

There are five principles to consider and questions to ponder as you enter the design stage:

1. *Top of mind, problem, pain or aspiration (TOMPPA):* For a business to be viable, it needs to address a significant enough problem, or attractive enough aspiration, for people to be motivated to invest their time, attention, energy and money. This is where your experience, opinions and interests often combine.

   As mentioned earlier, many next-chapter businesses are built on skinned knees: the business owner has overcome challenges and now has insights that can shorten and sweeten the similar journeys of others. This is a core premise underpinning my own mentoring now. I don't want to see other business owners staying stuck and potentially miserable in a business that no longer fits them for a moment longer than they need to.

Spend time understanding the needs of the audience you want to serve. Look for the point where those needs intersect with your interests and potential services. Do they have both the motivation and the means to invest in a solution that will address their TOMPPA?

2. *Service:* Your business needs to complement rather than commandeer your life, serving you as much as you serve your clients. This will decrease the chance of burnout and resentment, and increase the chance of sustainability. There will definitely be times within your business life when you're working harder than usual, but if this becomes the norm it's a sure sign that something needs to change.

Take time to consider and map out how your business will dovetail with your life. A business can quickly dominate both your thoughts and your life if you allow it to. You can find yourself thinking about it 24/7 and not clocking off the way you would if you were employed; however, this needn't be a problem if you love what you do and have clear value-based boundaries in place.

For example, I choose not to work in December and January. This is when I want time to recharge and fully focus on my family, and so the personal programs I offer begin in February and finish at the end of November.

It's also important to set boundaries for when and how you'll be available to your clients in minor ways, such as daily opening hours, answering emails and taking calls.

3. *Your strengths:* Building a business based on your strengths is a smart strategy. Working with what comes easily to you will make the business-building process easier. Things will flow with less effort when you're utilising the strengths at the heart of your services, products and delivery methodology.

    There are many different quizzes and tests available to formally discover your strengths, beyond your own observations and experiences. I particularly like the Clifton Strengths Finder assessment,[17] which provides not only a snapshot of your key strengths and how they express themselves individually, but also how they work together.

    When you're aware of what your strengths are, the next step is to work out what they look like in action. My key strengths include positivity, ideation, empathy, synthesis and communication. I see ideation and synthesis in action when I'm working in strategy sessions and workshops, and at retreats. This is when I create new ideas, and help my clients clarify and expand their own ideas in an atmosphere of positivity and empathy. These are some of my happiest places in business.

4. *Your values:* To live and work feeling supported and in flow, energised and fulfilled, you need to be in alignment with your values. This is when you know what you stand for, what you believe and what you want for your clients. You might manage to keep going

for some time, especially if you tend towards stubbornness like me, but without this sense of connection and harmony, resentment and sadness will take over. I know, I've been there.

I've had ample time to reflect since I closed my agency. When I looked more closely at the structure of my business, I realised that some of my core values had been sidelined as I focused on scaling and the subsequent need to generate an increasingly higher turnover to cover costs. Although I hadn't become ruthless, my natural states of generosity, simplicity, and connection felt more difficult to prioritise when I had to be so utterly bottom-line focused.

Seeing your values on paper, and understanding what they mean to you, is a great start. The next step is to weave them into the heart of your business. For this you need to become aware of what they look like in action, and then anchor those actions into your daily activities and incorporate them into the core design of your business.

There is a comprehensive list of values in the appendix, where you can select the ones that most resonate with you. I recommend working with no more than six if you can. From there, explore what they look like in action, and how you will implement them into your business. For example, my value of generosity is in action with the free content, resources and experiences I provide to my community. I love providing this; it feels really good to me.

5. *Evolution:* I guarantee that the business you start today won't be the one you have in three, five or ten years' time, and that's exactly as it should be. I encourage you to think of your business growth in horizons: what you will do now, next, and later, with the

full understanding that what your 'later' entails will become clear once you're in motion. Expectations are one of the more capricious aspects of business, and so I encourage you to hold your intentions loosely and commit to responding thoughtfully to whatever appears for you on this journey.

When I began my marketing agency way back in 2003, I didn't anticipate my eventual move from consulting to mentoring. In the same way, I didn't see how important the concept of helping women connect to their innate self-worth, so they can take confident and consistent action on their goals, would become to me. Building a business is the deepest personal development journey you will embark upon and it's a constant evolution. You only need to see and take the first few steps. The rest of the adventure will unfold as you do.

QUESTIONS TO DEFINE YOUR FUTURE

To help you develop further clarity on the business you want to create, here are some key questions to consider and journal on:

- *What stage of life am I in?* Consider what's possible for you right now. I'm about to enter a new stage of life—the empty nest—and that will open a whole new horizon of possibility for me with regards to the time I will have for my business. There will be options, including regular travel, that were not available when my children were younger and needed more hands-on care.
- *What role do you want this business to play in your life?* Does it feel like a part-time priority, a full-time focus, a passion project, your legacy, or something else? Expect this to change

over time, but right now ask yourself what focus feels both possible and right for you.

- *Does it feel like a local, nationwide or international venture?* This decision will impact the way you set things up and choose to market, from the simple ideas of securing a .com or a com.au domain, renting office space, settling on pricing, to developing local area promotions and a communications schedule.

- *How many hours a week do you want to work? A month? A year?* Again, this may depend on the time your current stage of life allows you to invest in your business. The business may ask for more of your time in the initial set-up and establishment phase, but your choice is a personal preference and involves your desire for a business that fits around your life rather than a life that fits around your business.

- *Who do you want to serve and help? Why?* Often a TOMMPA is experienced by more than one group of people, and you will likely be more drawn to one than another. Perhaps both the leaders of charities and the leaders of corporations need help with creating and delivering impactful presentations, but you're drawn to the former because of your values and personal experiences.

- *Why are you uniquely capable to help these people with this issue?* You may have heard how important it is for people to know, like and trust you before they will consider working with you or buying from you. All three of these things are important. But there's something even more important: people need to be seen, heard and understood.

Your sense of empathy, for truly understanding what your audience is experiencing, is the quality that will most deeply connect you to them. This is why your most aligned clients often resemble you, as you were a few years ago, before you worked through the challenge they are now facing. Be clear on your own story and don't be afraid to share it, so people can see themselves in it.

- *How do you want to deliver your services and/or products?* The variations here are endless. In a service-based business, options include online self-study programs, online or in-person group programs, one-on-one coaching, and retreats and conferences delivered solely by yourself or in collaboration with others. I provide more guidance with these options later in this chapter.

- *What people and/or experiences have you had that have positively impacted you, and how would you like to share them with your own audience?* Spend some time considering the people in your life who have lifted you up, believed in you, and opened doors or new ways of thinking, and blend that with experiences that have stood out for you, providing growth, ease and aha moments. Have there been standout moments for you? When? What happened? How could these be adapted and incorporated into your business?

Answering these questions helped me understand that I wanted to develop long-term relationships with my clients rather than short-term transactions. Today this is deeply woven into my business heart. One of my central services involves masterminds for businesswomen, where I get to wrap each participant in unwavering emotional and strategic support. These are small, cohesive circles of four to six women who work together over ten months. They meet every fortnight, connect regularly in a private online community whenever they need help, encouragement or to celebrate, and spend time together at an in-person retreat each year.

Spending such extended periods of time together is fertile ground for developing deep connections, and the relationships that are built between the members of each group are joyful and deeply supportive.

This has become my favourite way of working. Masterminds have their roots in my experiences in the recovery movement. I like to say that I was 'loved back to life' by being in these circles of support. Groups of women and men provided me with their experience, strength and hope, passing on what they had learned, just as others had supported them. When I was designing my new business structure, I knew I wanted to bring aspects of this experience into my own work.

What feels equally as good to you? What components will you blend to create a combination of contribution, fulfilment and financial reward that's unique to you? It's vital to understand at this stage that there is no definitive way to design your business. There's no right way, there's just the right way for you.

THE ALTERNATIVE TO FORMULAS

'I'm feeling completely overwhelmed,' Belinda told me with a sigh. 'I feel like there's a mountain of work I have to do. I've been downloading all sorts of resources, watching webinars, getting on lists and taking all these courses to find the answers, the right way through, but it's just making me more confused. I'm seeing what everyone else is doing and it's paralysing me. It's just not me, all this push, push, push. I can't work this way. I don't think I'm cut out for this. Surely there's an easier way.'

Belinda is a classic next-chapter businesswoman, someone who had decided to take her experience, interests and deep desire to help others and channel these skills into a business. She has a huge heart, loads of talent and the ability to make a real difference for her clients, but she was in danger of giving up before she'd ever really begun. She was being sucked into the cacophony of noise and directives that surrounds us all every day in a world that is increasingly developed and delivered online.

Perhaps you've fallen victim to a similar malaise. Believing that there are predetermined and definitive ways in which to design, build and grow a business has stopped many women from stepping into their next chapter. Feeling decidedly icky about sales and marketing, feeling overwhelmed by all of the options, feeling intimidated by technical demands, feeling that you've left it too late and that your ideas are too small or too big—there are a myriad of ways in which the dominant business culture and your risk-averse inner critic might discourage you from starting or growing your own business.

It's not surprising that with the sheer volume of information on offer today we can often default to the apparent relief that a formula seems to provide:

Feeling frustrated, overwhelmed and disappointed? Finding it hard to achieve financial success? Do it this way. Follow these steps and it will all work out in record time. It worked for me.

Such a promise is naturally enticing, but the problem is that a formula is ultimately like a straitjacket. You can feel quite supported and relieved when you first put it on, but it's not long before you begin to realise that it only allows you to move in very particular ways and suddenly it doesn't feel so good anymore.

What's more, formulas often deliver a second punch to your confidence. If you still can't make things work with the formula at hand it can make you feel even worse. *What's wrong with me? All those other people made it work. Why can't I?*

I haven't been immune to the Pied Piper of formulas during my time as a business owner. I can only share this perspective because in the past I've been lured by the promise of a paint-by-numbers solution proffered by a mega-successful entrepreneur, and with hope in my heart have purchased their course or methodology and tried my very best to follow it.

I remember thinking that my Your Next Chapter community, my private Facebook group, wasn't as engaged as it 'should be'. From where did I draw that insight? From deep inside the comparison trap as I looked at other groups and decided that mine did not measure up. Eager to fix this perceived problem, I invested in a solution that offered hyper engagement and an effortless and endless flow of leads.

I dived into the content and began to implement the recommendations, but found myself completely disconnecting from the philosophies by step four of the process. It didn't sit well with me. Nothing was immoral or underhanded, but the strategies felt incongruous to me, out of alignment with the way I liked to show up in the world. The system worked for the woman who created it because it was in alignment with her, but it was not designed for me so how could I possibly expect it to fit me equally well?

The simple reality is that formulas ultimately restrict your innate creativity, individuality and intuition, three of the most important tools you have available to you as a businesswoman. Formulas homogenise you into a pre-packaged cookie batter, instead of allowing you to be a blend of the individual ingredients that will ensure you create a recipe for a business that's as unique as you. So rather than try to take the entire A-Z of someone else's formula, drawn from their unique experiences, and expect to have it perfectly fit your unique circumstances, let's consider the alternative.

I'm a huge believer in the power of frameworks rather than formulas when it comes to the design stage of Your Next Chapter. You are most likely to thrive when you allow yourself the freedom to blend and combine select aspects of existing models using your own innate ideas, creating a mix that works for you.

Frameworks are concepts and approaches that provide you with guidance and assistance: parameters to work within so you feel neither strictly dictated to nor left to assemble the business design puzzle without having an image of what you're trying to build. Think of a framework as the base ingredients into which you add your own vision, skills, experience, values and desires to create a sustainable, delicious meal, rather than just subsisting on the mechanics of business.

A formula will state: *Here's your suit in plain navy blue. The skirt must sit exactly two inches above your knee and be worn with low court heels.*

A framework will state: *Clothing is essential, of course, but please feel free to choose the style that feels good to you, fits your frame, feels easy to move in, and is in a colour that flatters you.*

A framework encourages you to consider and be inspired by existing business models. It enables you to select the ones that feel right to you, adding your own variations and creating something brand new that is tailored perfectly for you.

With this in mind, let's take a look at business models operating today that are likely choices for you. You can then see how you could combine aspects of those into your own freedom framework.

YOUR FREEDOM FRAMEWORK

In its simplest form, a business model is a description of how you create and deliver value for your clients or customers, with the business receiving a value exchange in return, i.e. a financial reward.

Traditionally, every business model has three core components:

1. Processes that relate to designing and developing product/s or service/s.
2. Processes involved in selling and delivering a product/s or service/s.
3. Processes that cover how customers and clients will pay, and how the business (and the owner) will generate revenue and make a profit.

I like to add a fourth component:

4. Processes that relate to the purpose of the business, ensuring a sense of connection, growth, fulfilment and meaning for the customer or client and the owner.

Many years ago, the old sales model of business had us create a product or service, take it out into the world and convince people that they needed it. Then, we were told, people would buy.

We then moved onto the marketing model, which assured us that it was better to first find the need in the market before creating a product or service that met that need and taking it out into the world. We needed to demonstrate and communicate how and why what we had was a better solution than what was currently available. Then, we were told, people would buy.

Today, the marketing model is still pursued, but it seems to have become a great deal more complicated, with a plethora of twists and turns. The focus now is often on predicting emerging needs, or better still, actually creating those new needs. We need to remind people of their pain and fears, to trigger feelings of FOMO (fear of missing out) envy and insecurity. Then, we are told, people will buy. If they don't, we have to shout louder and hustle harder. Advertise. Build our list. Create sales funnels. Cut prices. Be active on all the social-media platforms. Eventually we'll get our slice of the market, our market share.

And then we scale, because bigger is better, and we all want to grow our customer base and revenue, don't we? This is the Holy Grail of business success, right?

If reading those descriptions leaves you feeling a little ill, you're not alone. If it feels as though the social-media age has made it almost impossible to be heard in an increasingly boisterous environment, as though the core of business, of serving and being rewarded for the service you provide, has been usurped by smoke and mirrors, hustle and push, push, push, please take heart. Yes, the world has changed, but there is always room and demand for genuine, authentic services and products.

The marketing platforms available to us today have the potential to provide amazing visibility and connection opportunities. It's when we believe we must design our business models and tap into these marketing tools in a particular, restrictive, formulaic way that we can trip ourselves up.

There is a small range of options when it comes to the core components of business models (franchise or network marketing options aside). It's the unique way in which you choose to build and deliver your ideas that adds to the incredible variety of businesses we see. Consider the modules below to be building blocks that you piece together into a simple framework or a more complex blend that encompasses all of the ways in which you want to deliver your work.

- Products: Manufacture your own.
- Products: Distribute someone else's.
- Retailer: Sell products in a physical store.
- Retailer: Sell products online in an e-commerce store.
- Service provider: Deliver services face to face.
- Service provider: Deliver services online.
- High touch: Provide an intimate, personalised experience.
- Low touch: Provide a broader, more financially accessible experience.

With a freedom framework you create the business that fits *you*, taking into account the stage of life you are at, your goals, skills, experience, values and personal interests. What do you desire to create? What would feel good to you, and serve the people and market you're called towards?

Whatever combination you select, develop and deliver, the key is to meet the intersection of desire and need between you and your client so you can both benefit.

As a perfect example, one of my beautiful mentoring clients has an eclectic business that combines five of the core components into her freedom framework:

- High touch: Personal, one-to-one mentoring
- Online: Delivered via Zoom
- Manufacture: Creates her own products to sell
- E-commerce: Sells her own products through her website
- Distributor: Sells other people's products through her website

Another client has a very simple framework involving manufacturing and e-commerce, wherein she creates and sells her gorgeous aromatherapy mists through her website. Others focus on intimate high-touch service models, delivering consulting, training and coaching services face to face and online as HR and PR consultants.

My own business also has a freedom framework: I'm a service provider offering intimate high-touch, online, and low-touch options:

- Intimate high touch: I facilitate small group masterminds, VIP days, and retreats where each participant has my personal attention on their business and challenges. These are intimate rather than large-audience experiences.
- Online: In my business, online refers to the fact that I have no office as such, with much of my mentoring delivered via the video-conferencing platform Zoom.

- Low touch: Your Journey Board is a self-study program, accessible through my Your Next Chapter hub course library. With pre-recorded audios as my clients' connection point, there is less personal interaction with me than through my other programs.

As you can see, the options really are endless when you step into the freedom framework.

A PURPOSEFUL START

At the start of your journey, identify a simple need in the world that you are passionate about providing a genuine solution to, a connection born of empathy, experience and expertise.

When I say expertise, I don't mean that you should wait until you know every aspect of your chosen industry or profession (unless your passion is something like surgery, in which case, please do). This seemingly productive procrastination robs the world of so much talent and potential. Please don't fall into the same trap.

Your clients, the people you're here to connect with and help, are not looking for polished perfection. They don't want a guru preaching to them from a mountaintop. They want you to come down into the trenches with them and sit with them. They want to be seen, heard and understood. They want you to take their hand, look them in the eye and say, 'It's okay. I understand. I've been here and I know the way through.' And then they want you to guide them through and out.

And believe me, they're not likely to ask to see your formal qualifications when you're deftly helping them through what they're experiencing as a painful, challenging obstacle. To be of service, all you need to be is a few steps ahead in experience.

I see the world as a continuum, not a hierarchy. I don't see people above or below me. I simply see people ahead who started before me and who then turn around and offer their help, insights, experience and service to people like you and me, who are coming along behind them. We then, in turn, do the same for those behind us. I love the image that conjures up for me, and I trust you can see the truth in it, too.

So please relax. The biggest lesson here for you is to lean into self-trust.

You have what it takes to get started, and you will hone your clarity and skills further as you're moving. Don't wait for the perfect time. Take the time you have now, make a perfectly wonderful start, and then allow your enthusiasm to create momentum as your experience builds.

At this stage in the cycle of change, I've found it's important to gently connect once again to the concept of purpose or being purposeful. We could add to that, vision and mission. This combination provides you with a clear focus and filter for making decisions.

I draw upon the work of my good friend Carolyn Tate, author of *The Purpose Project*,[18] when it comes to defining these three concepts:

- *Purpose:* Start in your heart, rather than your head, because purpose is the heartbeat of your business. It drives vision, mission and values, addressing why you do what you do. It's your guiding north star and can feel spiritually influenced. It's always deeply personal.

- *Vision:* Your vision is what the world looks like when your purpose is being realised. It influences and directs your day-to-day activities.
- *Mission:* This is how you get from purpose to vision; it's your quest. It's all about what you do and the path you take to realise your *why*.

Like your business as a whole, your purpose, vision and mission will also evolve over time, just as you do. At the time of writing—mid 2020—this is how I define mine. I have no doubt that by the time you're reading this book it will have morphed a little again, because I emphasise how important it is to be purposeful in your work, rather than being perfectly on purpose.

- *Purpose:* To reconnect women with their innate self-worth so they can take confident and consistent action on their vision and goals.
- *Vision:* Thousands of women owning their worth and leveraging their experience, strengths and insights in businesses that positively impact the world.
- *Mission:* To provide women with inspiration, support and guidance to build sustainable businesses and lives that blend contribution, fulfilment and financial reward through resources, events and programs.

I have these statements displayed on a corkboard in my office, and I focus on them when I have wobbly days. When I need to make a choice or a decision, I focus on them. When I'm trying to decide if I'm facing an opportunity or a distraction, I focus on them. These anchors provide a filter that helps me to see more clearly if the thing in question aligns with my purpose, if it will take me towards or away from my vision, and if it keeps me on mission or sends me off on a tangent. Bright, shiny options can be tantalising, and so the ability to recognise and then sidestep or resist those baubles is valuable.

I've supported many of my clients in creating their own statements so they can be anchored on the stormy days they will invariably face. I offer here a couple of my favourites that I trust will serve as inspiration as you create your own.

The first is from Time Rich, a partnership of two women, Emma and Andrea, who are transforming the traditional face of productivity and time management. Their philosophy is coloured and influenced by having faced deep grief, and as a result developing a new relationship with time. I have goosebumps when I read this; it feels so true and important.

- *Purpose:* To help people deeply appreciate the beauty and fragility of life so they live fully, richly and courageously without regret.
- *Vision:* People consciously and consistently making choices and decisions that enrich their lives each day.
- *Mission:* To support our community and clients to develop the beliefs, habits and courage that allow them to create and shape lives they love.

Another one I love is from Mags, the founder of Sober Mojo, a coaching service for women who find themselves newly sober, are a little uncertain about what that means, and are looking for help to navigate the new landscape they find themselves in. I love the work she is doing.

- *Purpose:* To shine a light on women's inner power so they put themselves first, reach their potential, and live a full and fabulous life in recovery.
- *Vision:* A world where women have no need to numb themselves because they've connected to their inner power, have complete self-acceptance, and use their voices freely and honestly to build full and fabulous lives.
- *Mission:* To equip women with the skills, tools and self-knowledge to connect to their inner power and know that life is now limitless for them.

Are you ready to play with your own statements? Turn to your journal and see what bubbles to the surface for you. Creating the first draft is your goal; you will certainly refine it once you are in motion.

THE PROGRESSIVE ENGAGEMENT PLAN

Once the core of your business is beginning to take shape in your head and heart, there are many more practical considerations to dive into. These include your branding, website, pricing, and marketing and communications plans. Although this book is not intended as a how-to guide (that would double its size), I'll now walk you through a framework that many of my clients have found useful in helping them to clarify their thoughts, and focus their energy and attention at the business design or redesign stage.

A progressive engagement plan (PEP) is a framework for the series of interactions a potential client has with you as they progress from discovering you, to engaging with you, to transforming into a paying client or customer, and ultimately referring you to other people who can also benefit from your work.

There are seven steps involved and I use the acronym DEEEPER, which is fitting since it's about developing deep client relationships over time.

D: Discover

E: Engage

E: Educate

E: Elevate

P: Progress

E: Embrace

R: Recommend and refer

Step 1: Discover

This is when you become visible so that your potential clients and customers can find you. There are so many ways in which you can be discovered, but they basically fall into three key areas:

- Online: Primarily through a website; one of the many social-media platforms (Facebook, Instagram, Linked In etc.); a virtual event or community (webinar, interview, Telesummit, Facebook group); or other medium like a podcast, YouTube channel, guest blog post or article submission
- Third-party: Through a referral from a delighted client or colleague
- In person: When you attend or speak at conferences and events, large and small

Rest assured that you won't have to employ all of these options, which would be exhausting. Instead, start with just one or two that you find joyful. What do you love to do? Write beautiful, compelling copy? Interview people? Create online communities? Shine on a stage?

With a wholehearted marketing approach, you work with what comes easily to you because it means you're far more likely to implement consistently: it's consistency that increases the likelihood of you being seen and heard as you demonstrate your understanding of the challenges your audience is experiencing and how you can help.

I want to encourage you to always be yourself when you market your business. This is not about convincing and converting people; rather, it's about contributing and communicating, and consistently adding value, in your style, to the world. I like to think about this as sharing ideas and content that pops, weaving together your:

- Perspective
- Philosophies
- Opinions
- Stories

The content, resources, events and experiences you develop and share pop when you are open, vulnerable, authentic and honest, being unequivocally yourself. This is when your most genuine connections will be made. Since we're focused on building a sustainable business on the foundation of long-term relationships with clients, rather than short-term transactions with customers, this approach makes perfect sense.

There are literally hundreds of thousands of business mentors and coaches in the world, but there is only one me, with my unique point of view and combination of experiences, just as there is only one you.

As I've become increasingly comfortable with showing up as me, in the ways that come naturally to me, it's only the people who are already resonating with my style, ideas and perspectives who contact me or are referred to me. These are the clients who are a delight to work with, because we are closely aligned in our thinking, values, and beliefs, and they frequently become good friends. I encourage you to be similarly open and authentically you and enjoy the relationships you'll build as a result.

Step 2: Engage

Once someone has discovered you and your work, and they feel aligned with your message, the next step is to invite them into your world by offering a simple solution to an aspect of the TOMMPA (top of mind problem, pain or aspiration) they're experiencing.

This often involves an exchange of value: your guidance, information and insight for their contact details so you can deliver your solution snippet to them. This is often referred to as an opt-in or lead magnet and comes in a myriad of forms. Common examples include:

- E-books
- Webinars
- Quizzes and tip sheets
- Videos
- Discount coupons
- Online community

Again, choose an option that feels easeful and appealing for you, and that offers true value to your audience. Stay aligned with the 'seen, heard and understood' philosophy I introduced earlier. Imagine an individual downloading, reading or watching your opt-in and feeling real relief and delight, knowing they've found someone who understands and is offering the first step to a true solution.

There's no need to reinvent the wheel here. You can create one fabulous thing and then offer it happily across all of the discovery activities you've chosen.

I know that one thing my own audience can struggle with is building the confidence to pursue their business vision, especially if they work alone. I also understand the immense power of example. My e-book and audio book, *Increase Your Confidence and Self-Worth*, shares short stories and the insights of seventeen businesswomen who have created their own businesses, alongside a host of my own confidence-building principles and tools. It is a valuable resource that I have freely offered on my website and social-media platforms for more than five years.

What might be of value for your audience? Sometimes a lead magnet is not the right fit for the market you're seeking to engage. A corporate client may be more inclined to make a direct approach after finding your work, checking your profile on LinkedIn, or being referred. I've also had new clients skip over my incentives and simply message me.

Make sure the issues you address and the outcomes you create are clear and compelling, and the ways to get in touch with you are obvious to facilitate these fast-action people.

Step 3: Educate

Everyone moves through their own buying cycle when they're trying to solve a problem or realise an aspiration. Sometimes this cycle is simple and short and doesn't require a lot of consideration. *I'm thirsty and want a drink, so I'll pop into a store and grab one.* But a choice can often involve lengthy deliberation when you're in the midst of a more significant investment, like weighing up the pros and cons of one car over another, planning an itinerary for an overseas holiday, or choosing a website developer.

Some of my own clients tell me they followed me online for a number of years before they were ready to get in touch. This is in direct contrast to others who tell me they just stumbled across my website. They felt as though I was talking directly to them and they felt they had to contact me right away.

This considerable variation is why the 'educate' part of your PEP involves sharing insights, resources and tools that add value and allow people the time and opportunity they need to move through their own buying cycle, at their own speed.

Yes, there are actions that can shorten the journey, encouraging quicker responses. But a simple focus on providing value, choosing to demonstrate your understanding and experience through activities such as blog posts, videos, podcasts, resources, challenges, newsletters and online communities will give them the chance to get to know you, what you stand for and the ways in which you can help them to address their TOMMPA.

I like to think of marketing and communication tactics in two categories: marketing megaphones, which involve significant time and planning, and marketing support acts, which are easier, more everyday actions.

My megaphones for example, are my podcast, Next Chapter dinners, and now this book. My support acts are my social-media activities, including my private Facebook community, networking on and offline, and my newsletter.

An important reminder: again, don't try to spread yourself thinly across too many activities. The most effective marketing tool is consistency, and that's a difficult commitment to make when you're under self-imposed pressure. Don't adhere to a demanding formula; instead, develop your own easeful, consistent rhythm.

Step 4: Elevate

This is an exciting step. This is when someone makes the move from being a potential client to becoming an actual paying client. It's important to appreciate that any client who chooses to work with you, purchase one of your products or attend an event has likely already invested their time, energy and attention in your work by listening, reading, learning from and being inspired by you. Now they've made the decision to invest financially as well, and with so many options available to them, gratitude is a great energy for you to be grounded in at this stage.

The elevate step is often offered as a relatively low-risk investment, perhaps a single session, short program or small product. With online, service-based businesses, this can also be a self-study DIY scenario, often without personal interaction beyond video or audio. But in every case, a client has a positive experience of your skills and style, your solutions and your approach, which can lead to the decision to invest in a longer-term relationship with you.

As I write, my personal strategy sessions represent the 'elevate' step in my business.

Step 5: Progress

This is a significant turning point, when you have a wholehearted conversation with an aligned client to explore if there is a good fit between their challenges and your solutions, their vision and your skills. It's also a time to demonstrate how you can be useful and add value to their world in a significant way. It's most common when someone has either been following you for some time and decides to get in touch, or has invested in one of your smaller services or programs, enjoyed it, and realised they need more of your help to reach their goals.

Because you've been consistent and committed to showing up authentically as you work through the discover, engage, educate and elevate steps, these fruitful discussions are more likely to take place with people who are already aligned with you, leading to enjoyable, engaged conversations and connected, positive outcomes. I recommend giving this expansive conversation a distinct name that communicates to a potential client the valuable outcome they will experience. I call mine 'a next-chapter breakthrough call'.

Step 6: Embrace

I like to think of this next stage of the blossoming client relationship as when you embrace one another, when your client has made the powerful decision to invest in and commit to their own transformation and service intimacy with you. This is the realm of VIP days, group programs, retreats, masterminds, and one-on-one coaching and mentoring, at investment levels that truly reflect the value you will bring to their businesses and lives.

Step 7: Recommend and refer

Once your clients have embraced you, they often become advocates and referral partners, which is a delightful, joyful, humbling and fulfilling experience. We've all experienced the power of a personal referral and how the transfer of trust it represents can quickly establish connection and speed up the decision-making process.

This PEP framework is intended to provide you with gentle guidance as you grow and expand your ideas, confidence and experience. No two plans are ever the same, but they do tend to share one core commonality: they are simple at the outset, most often with just one action item or offer at each step, and become more complex over time as your business grows.

The design of your business is ultimately in your hands, and you have the freedom and creativity to create the framework and model that works best for you and your audience. Play with your ideas. Test and try things out. One of the best things about being a solo or small-business owner is your ability to be nimble, to see how something works and feels, and to make changes or expand based on the feedback you receive both from your clients and your own emotions. That's a freedom framework in action.

There's another thought to ponder as you design your next chapter, one that I trust will compel you to embrace your unique perspective, to not tone down how you feel and the impact you want to have in the world. It's something I call the 'rule of thirds'.

Imagine you have carefully and wholeheartedly crafted a message about your business, what you stand for and believe in, and want for your clients, and you've displayed this message on a huge billboard in Times Square. It's strong, it's clear, it's brave; it *pops*.

A third of the people who walk by and pause to read your message consider it, shrug their shoulders and walk away, indifferent, with no feeling of connection or interest. That's absolutely fine. Let them go. Farewell them with love. There might be another billboard waiting around the corner that's just right for them.

The next third will arrive, stand in judgment of your message with hands on hips and dismiss it as rubbish, wrong, and possibly even ridiculous or offensive. That, too, is absolutely fine. Farewell this group with just as much love so they can find the billboard that has the right message for them.

But for the final group—your people, your third of the world—your message will bring them to a standstill. They will be captivated, hopeful, intrigued, relieved, excited, awakened, thrilled, fired up and inspired. They will know they've found their billboard, their solution, their person.

It's not your job to convince or convert the whole world or even the whole market to your way of thinking, your services or your business. It's your job to share your approach and solution openly, consistently, confidently and wholeheartedly; to focus on being useful and adding value to the world, your way; to trust that the right people for you will make the connection and that their next chapter will improve exponentially, because of you.

Let's take this business you've designed out into that world. Let's make you and your ideas visible so the people who are waiting for you can find you and experience that promise.

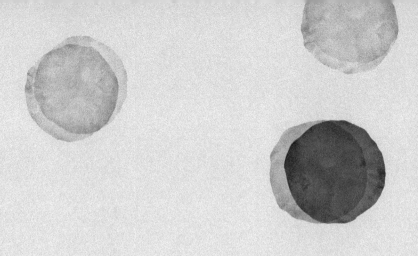

'If you have knowledge,
let others light their
candles in it.'

Margaret Fuller

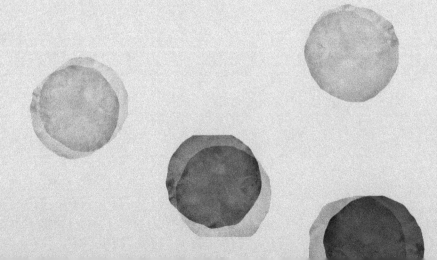

CHAPTER 6

DELIVER

Share Your Insights

'Oh, no, look at that,' my daughter whispered to me. 'Elphaba's makeup has rubbed off on Fiyeros face.'

For a moment, the two of us were distracted, mesmerised by the bright green smears on the actor's face that had been transferred during a passionate kiss. It was a small hiccup in the middle of a brilliant opening night of the musical *Wicked*, staged by our local theatre company. A few seconds later we were drawn back into the rollicking story and had forgotten all about it. The actors themselves seemed equally unfazed, and though there may have been a moment of panic when the renegade makeup was first spotted, the show did go on, and it was brilliant.

We can spend an enormous amount of time in rehearsal mode, getting every detail as close to perfect as possible, but there is still a chance something will go awry when we finally step out onto the stage. That's the nature of life. It's unpredictable.

But just like in the production Charlotte and I enjoyed so much, if an unexpected twist or two does occur, it seldom detracts from the overall positive experience of the participants or the audience. Our imaginations, however, fuelled by our internal critics, can try to tell us a vastly different story.

Launching or relaunching your business and delivering your products and services—releasing your ideas into the world—means taking a significant step, and it comes complete with a set of swirling emotions. It's not surprising, then, that moving from development and discussion, testing and tweaking your new or redefined business into the actual reality of hanging out your shingle and asking for the sale is a prime time for doubts and fears to resurface.

Being aware of the common obstacles you may find yourself facing at this stage is helpful because it means you'll be prepared to navigate through them if they try to wrap themselves around your ankles.

Until you actually put your ideas, services, offers and products out into the world, you don't know how they will be received. You have hope. You have dreams. You have the best of intentions about the potential of their positive impact. And you also have safety.

If you stay in the realm of potential, where you can imagine your ideas transforming effortlessly into accolades, success and dollars in the bank, the risks associated with exposing yourself never come to pass. If no one sees you or your ideas, you stay safe, with no judgment, no disapproval, no disappointment, and no need to face your fears. You never have to try to prove your inner critic wrong. There's no need to learn how to work through criticism, imposter syndrome, the comparison trap or heaven forbid, failure.

Instead, you can forever dine safely on stories of projection and imagination, of how wonderful it might be, could be, would be to step out in faith and contribute to the world in the way you're most called to do.

Let me share a secret with you. I've failed. Many times. Many, many times. So many times, it's simply not possible to recount them all.

I've launched programs no one has enrolled in. I've written blog posts and social-media posts that no one has ever commented on. I've recorded podcast episodes that very few people have listened to. I've planned and promoted events that no one booked a ticket for. I've hosted webinars for non-existent audiences; forgotten to hit record; and showed the wrong slides. I've lost contracts to competitors. I've had potential clients choose other mentors. I've had applications for award submissions ignored.

But I've also facilitated programs, workshops and retreats that have changed lives. I've created posts and resources that have been shared hundreds of times. I've released podcast episodes that have been downloaded thousands of times. I've hosted sold-out events, secured contracts, served more clients than I can count, and even won an award or two. I've felt my heart expand wider than I ever thought possible. I've met people who have become friends for life, and I've stretched and grown and deepened in ways I could never have anticipated.

And none of these things, not a single one, would have been possible if I'd stayed safe in the realm of potential. Instead, I continue to remind myself to consciously choose to be anchored by my self-worth, to connect to courage, to step out of what's familiar and safe and teeter along the edge of a new possibility.

Take this book, for example. For as long as I can remember I have harboured a fantasy of lurking in a store, watching someone pick up a book I've written, look at the cover, scan the back, flick through a few pages, read a little snippet here and there. Nod. Close it. Take it to the counter and buy it.

A lot of people have told me over the years that I should write a book. I would smile and say it was a great idea. But I've been too afraid to do it. Why? Because I felt I could never be the author I wanted to be in my head. It was safer, infinitely safer, to stay in the realm of potential; I could be a phenomenal potential author.

But you know what? I'm feeling more courageous now, and I decided I was going to be an author, whatever shape, style or form that took.

So please take a moment to breathe out fear, breathe in faith and step forward into one of the biggest growth experiences you could possibly imagine. You'll be amazed to discover who else you are in the process.

YOU CAN'T STEER A PARKED CAR

Something not going according to plan, something 'failing' is an experience to learn from. When it happens, you dust yourself off, harvest the lessons, provide yourself with a healthy dose of self-compassion, let go, adjust and move on. This is how you build resilience, empathy and knowledge.

You can't steer a parked car; you have to be in motion to change direction when an obstacle appears in front of you, and the more obstacles you get to see, the smarter you become. The more resilient you become, the more empathy you develop and the more insights you have to share because, as part of the Franklin Roosevelt quote made infinitely more famous by Brené Brown states, you are 'in the arena, daring greatly'.

To reach this point of delivery you will have done a lot of work, both internally and externally. Whether you are starting something brand new or redefining an existing business, you may already have:

- A name for your business
- A home for your business online (website or social-media platform) or offline (perhaps a storefront or market stall)
- An offer or offers at a defined price point
- A methodology or system for delivering that offer
- A simple marketing/visibility/connection plan

Pause for a moment and recognise that you have actually created something from nothing. You've taken an idea, given it shape and form, and developed a means of adding value to the world in your own unique way. I want you to reverse gap yourself, to pause for a moment. Rather than focusing only on how far you still have to go, remember to appreciate how far you've come. Recognise that, no matter where you go from here, getting to this point is an achievement that an increasing, yet still relatively small, number of people in the world choose to do. A celebration is in order. How will you mark and commemorate your progress?

Elation and fear are understandable feelings at this stage in the process, and there are distinct actions you can take to honour one and calm the other. What can be unexpected, however, is the experience of simply running out of steam and energy, of having the finishing line in sight and not being able to get yourself across it.

It's important to know that hovering on the doorstep of a significant threshold will act as a classic trigger for your inner critic, so expect her to resurface. While you've been designing all the aspects of your business, developing your model and offers, creating catchy marketing ideas and the like, your inner critic has been pretty relaxed. Unthreatened.

When she realises, however, that all of this seemingly innocent activity is now leading somewhere public and exposed, she can be gripped by a panic spasm, go on high alert, and become exceedingly vocal and opinionated again. She is likely to leap up and begin to wag her finger and berate you, tossing emotional hand grenades in your path designed to stop you in your tracks. These grenades most commonly take the simple form of recycled doubts and comparison.

Here are some common inner-critic outbursts my clients have shared with me when they're at the threshold of delivery (many of which have been mirrored in the words of my very own Helga, in her most disdainful tone):

- *What on earth were you thinking?*
- *This is ridiculous, pointless, pathetic, actually.*
- *Surely you realise no one will be interested.*
- *No one will be stupid enough to spend money on that.*
- *Seriously? You're going to say that? Do that?*
- *And you think that's what people need. Really?*
- *Why are you bothering? No one's going to care.*
- *You do know that's already been done, don't you?*
- *You really haven't got a clue, have you?*

If your inner critic is a little sweeter, but ultimately still focused on keeping you small, safe and secure, she'll likely couch her sentiments in the softer, more devious tones of perfectionism and procrastination. These messages might initially appear somewhat kinder and more sensible:

- *Oh, it's so close, honey, but perhaps it just needs a little more. After all, you want to show your best self to the world, don't you?*

- *I'm not sure you're quite ready yet, sweetheart. Perhaps you should enrol in that course/program that you saw last week. It's better to be safe than sorry.*

- *Are you sure you've asked enough people what they think yet? After all, they are your potential customers, so their opinions are really important*

- *Oh, you have plenty of time for that. Have a break; you deserve it. There's no rush.*

If your inner critic can keep up a flow of negative dialogue or seemingly productive procrastination, she'll succeed in her task of keeping you umming and ahhing, polishing what already shines. She'll stop you from stepping out into what she sees as open season for entrepreneurs.

The delivery phase can be a genuinely scary time in negotiating your next chapter. But it can also be the most exhilarating, exciting, delightful period of your life when you step forward into a whole new way of being. This is why I love this quote from psychiatrist and founder of Gestalt therapy, Fritz Perls: 'Fear is only excitement without the breath.'

BEFRIEND YOUR EMOTIONS

As we briefly explored in the earlier chapter on doubt, adrenaline is released in response to stressful, exciting, dangerous, or anxiety-inducing situations, especially situations with uncertain outcomes. In other words, the kind of situations that business owners face fairly regularly.

Adrenaline is often called the fight-or-flight hormone because it readies the body for action, making the heart beat faster, increasing blood flow to the brain and muscles, and stimulating the body to produce a burst of sugar it can use for fuel. The rush of adrenaline begins in the brain, with the amygdala and hypothalamus. The adrenal glands respond to their messages by releasing adrenaline into the bloodstream, and in a split-second breathing and heart rate increase, the pupils dilate, the palms sweat, and the stomach drops. Your body is creating a landscape of stress, and your mind kicks in to deepen the angst.

Your inner critic is prompted by the sudden burst of adrenaline to jump up and start sharing her views. She has a lot to say. No wonder backing off and indulging in some other far less anxiety-inducing activity, like scrolling Facebook, working on a future content-creation schedule, or redesigning a logo or website becomes immensely appealing.

But the thing is, when you feel a far more attractive and useful emotion like excitement, your amygdala, hypothalamus and adrenal glands buddy up to trigger exactly the same physiological reactions. When you're excited, you're just as likely to experience your breathing and heart rate speeding up, your palms sweating and your stomach rolling around like a Ferris wheel. Fear and anxiety can shut you down, but excitement and anticipation can open you up, and they're right at your fingertips at the very same time.

How can you ensure you connect with these more energising emotions when you're on the edge of delivering your new ideas to the world? By thinking differently.

Assuming that opening or promoting your business doesn't actually put you in a life-or-death situation, the patterns of thought that you entertain and the way you decide to respond are pivotal. When the initial rush of adrenaline hits, and your stomach contracts or your throat closes with anxiety or fear, choosing a conscious response rather an automatic reaction will determine whether you open up and move forward, or shut down and turn away, essentially sabotaging yourself.

When you first become aware of what's happening in your body, you have the opportunity to change your emotional experience of the situation and therefore change what happens next. That's incredibly powerful. The work of Harvard Business School professor Allison Wood Brooks shows us exactly how to manage this. Surprisingly, trying to calm yourself down when you are on the delivery threshold is exactly what you should *not* do.

Dr Brooks' research showed that trying to shift from a state of high anxiety or perceived fear to a state of calm is incredibly challenging and even counterproductive.[19] Anxiety and fear are states of high physiological arousal, and they provide you with energy to harness and direct. Excitement is also a state of high arousal, and both states actually offer you energy to feast upon. The only real difference between these two conditions is the story your mind creates around them.

If you're travelling in the territory of fear and anxiety, you're future tripping, projecting yourself into a world where things go wrong, where you're judged harshly and come off wanting, where you say or do the wrong thing and look foolish, with people pointing and laughing at you. Contrast that with a trip into the territory of excitement, where you look forward to the adventure with eagerness and positivity, ready to be of service and to share your ideas, where you're focused on what can go right rather than what can go wrong.

It's so much easier, quicker and useful for you as a business owner in delivery mode to travel from fear and anxiety to excitement and anticipation, two outposts that are close together, than it is to try to traverse the yawning chasm that has calm certainty sitting on the other side.

When you try to calm yourself down in a new or challenging situation, you can hit good old-fashioned resistance and find it very difficult. Then you can become anxious about the fact that you're feeling anxious, continuing the entire, excruciating spiral.

This is not unlike piercing yourself with what is referred to as 'the second arrow' in Buddhist teachings. The first arrow is an actual unpleasant event, which can cause pain (our anxiety or fear response), and the second arrow is the suffering we attach to it. *I should be able to stop this, for goodness' sake. Everyone will see how scared I am. This is ridiculous. Why can't I stop this?* These responses are optional; they are your reaction to the event.

Dr Brooks found that when her subjects practised what she calls 'anxiety reappraisal', when they deliberately shifted from seeing tasks as threats to seeing them as opportunities, they performed better. In essence, they chose to change the story they were telling themselves, and that changed the response of their mind and focus and therefore their results.

The first time I hosted a webinar, my stomach, throat and critic joined forces and cooked up a massive anxiety feast, delivering it to me right before it was time to go live. As an extrovert, I gain much of my energy from connecting with people, being able to see and interact from the heart with my audience. A traditional webinar removed that opportunity and also handed me the challenge of mastering new technology, not always my strongest suit.

The nervous tension literally made me clumsy. I hit the wrong buttons, almost deleting the event. Helga began to taunt me, telling me that I'd never present half as well as any number of other entrepreneurs I'd watched online at that stage. She told me I'd probably screw it up completely and everyone on the call would think I was a total idiot.

I stood at a choice point. I could allow the adrenaline to strangle me, cancel the webinar and retreat into potato chips and self-recriminations, or I could reframe the trepidation and anxiety I was feeling with lashings of self-compassion. It took conscious choice and formidable focus to tell myself how exciting it was to develop this new skill, this new way of connecting with people. I regrouped, hit the start button and made it through, imperfectly, for sure, but that's how we all begin.

Like anything new, the strength of the reappraisal practice lies in repetition. The more often you choose to meet the emotions and experiences of fear and anxiety with this conscious response, rather than having a skittish reaction, the easier it will become to move confidently into anticipation and excitement when the situation demands it. Before you know it, you'll be bouncing through fear and anxiety with aplomb as your self-belief grows through the evidence of your ability to do so.

By the time you're reading this, I will have hosted hundreds of webinars, online master classes, and mentoring and mastermind sessions. Over the years I've tamed many new technologies, and actually now enjoy the benefits of working with technology and the opportunities it offers, but my stomach still lurches a little when it's time to show up. Fortunately, the reappraisal from fear to excitement is almost automatic these days, and Helga stays seated, knitting up a storm because this has become a familiar realm for us both.

You'll face many similar challenging growth edges on your business adventure and will learn the skills to deal with them in the moment. You'll also have the option of strengthening your confidence and self-belief with some preventative measures, which I'll share with you now so you can pop the ones that resonate into your own toolbox.

YOUR DAILY DIALOGUE

In the 1970s, Dr John Gottman and Dr Robert Levenson began studying couples' behaviours around handling conflict and challenges. They were able to predict which couples would happily stay together and which would divorce, with over ninety-percent accuracy.

What they discovered was simple and powerful, a ratio of positive and negative interactions during conflicts and challenges that appeared to contribute to strong and enduring relationships. There was a 'magic ratio' of 5 to 1: a secure and joyful marriage has at least five positives for every one negative interaction, comment or response.[20]

Of course, this book isn't intended as a marriage guide, and I'm certainly not a marriage counsellor, but I believe the good doctors' findings have relevance for you as a businesswoman. Having positive surrounding influences, a belief buddy (my name for someone who understands your goals and provides unstinting encouragement through all of your ups and downs), being a member of a formal or peer mastermind—these are all important and valuable to help keep you bouyant on your business journey.

But what happens when you leave the room? What happens when you end the phone call? What happens when you don't have these people in your hip pocket?

The truth is *you* are the person you'll spend the most time with on this adventure. You're the only person who will be there every day as you traverse each twist and turn of the business-building landscape. You need to consistently support yourself with that same ratio of positive to negative interactions to ensure the relationship you have with yourself is strong, consistent and supportive. And that's why I recommend developing a daily-dialogue practice.

Your daily dialogue is the mixture of gratitude, love, acceptance, encouragement and kindness that you direct towards yourself on a daily basis. Here's a simple equation to remind you of its impact:

$$DD \times C = LSE$$

Daily dialogue x consistency = (the) likelihood (of) successful endeavours

The likelihood of a successful endeavour (LSE), whatever your goal may be, is influenced by the consistency of your supportive daily dialogue. Knowing this, you can make a conscious decision to have positive, encouraging, kind, optimistic conversations with yourself, nourishing your sense of self-worth on a daily basis.

Start the moment you wake up in the morning, when you put your feet on the floor, when you see yourself in the mirror. Rather than standing by, ready to react when your inner critic lobs an emotional hand grenade in your direction, create a preventative practice in the spirit of 'an apple a day keeps the doctor away'.

When I looked back with the benefit of kindsight at my early weeks, months and years in sobriety, I realised just how important a part this practice had played in the gradual growth of my sense of optimism, capability, and value. It helped move me from a place of self-loathing, self-deprecation and negativity into a place of self-acceptance, self-support and, eventually, self-worth. This simple, loving commitment to myself was one of the disciplines that changed my life.

As my relationship with myself improved, a sense of unconditional support became available to me. I began to stretch myself, try new things, and step out of the restrictions of my previous comfort and familiar realm because I realised I had a safe place to land, no matter what the outcome of my actions. It allowed me to become bolder, and to develop a deep resilience and optimism encased in a joyful and playful relationship with myself that serves me to this day.

If every woman developed her own unique daily dialogue practice in a proactive and conscious way, the likelihood of having successful endeav-ours—sending a blog post out into the world, hosting a webinar, speaking on stage, unveiling a new brand, launching a new service, whatever her goal may be—would increase significantly.

And so I encourage you to create your own. It may feel a little foreign at first, this concept of speaking to yourself as though you're chatting with a friend but stick with it. I promise it's a game changer.

DEALING WITH EXPECTATIONS

Even in the midst of supportive conversations with yourself, it's important to understand the role that expectations play in your entrepreneurial world, and how they can trip you up and steal your confidence if you're not aware. An expectation is an assumption of how things should be, or, if you have been more tightly wound, of how things *must* be. These 'shoulds' and 'musts' hooking into you and demanding a predetermined outcome according to self-imposed deadlines and standards can be responsible for a lot of disappointment and pain.

Here are a few expectation experiences from my clients:

- This is such a fabulous newsletter. I can't wait to send it. I just know it's one of the best I've ever created. (But the opening rate turns out to be lower than usual on this occasion.)
- This offer is so good. It's going to be snapped up. (But very few people place an order on this day.)
- I've followed every step of the process and I'm going to have that same success. (But things don't flow in the same way.)
- This LinkedIn article is great. It's thought provoking, and it's going to kickstart a really animated discussion. (But no one leaves a comment.)

- I'm feeling really focused today. I'm going to be super-productive. (But the day seems to fly by, and your to-do list remains stubbornly unticked.)

The biggest expectation of all, which we are almost duty bound to bump up against is: *This is the way my business should, must, will grow.* Unfortunately, your internal timetable is not a prerequisite the world and the market will faithfully respond to. If your expectations, especially of rapid growth, are not met, it can wreak havoc on your confidence, and the self-recriminations can be hard to bear. By all means, set goals and work towards them, but hold them lightly, rather than tightly, in your heart because in business no one has a crystal ball.

Have you ever planned something for someone and been disappointed? Maybe you gave someone a special gift, telling yourself it was perfect, thinking the recipient would be delighted, and waited for their reaction. And they did seem happy, and did thank you, but you know them well and felt they were not as excited and grateful as they could or should have been. You didn't feel the appreciation you anticipated. Instead, you felt a little upset, a little annoyed and a little irritated.

Resentment bubbles up from deep inside. It's easy to see how potentially destructive the fallout of this cascade of emotions can be. In the recovery movement, we refer to expectations as 'premeditated resentments', and for good reason. Resentment is a feeling of displeasure and indignation that can morph into bitterness and acrimony when directed externally, and can turn into disappointment, blame and shame when used internally against yourself.

The way to break the expectation-resentment-recrimination cycle in business and life is to do great work with the best of intentions, and then to be unattached from the outcome, to launch and let go. It takes practice, which is why unconditional self-support is such a vital skill to build.

It's also important to understand the role that judgment plays in expectations, and how our judgments are often based on incorrect and incomplete facts when we don't have access to the complete picture.

Imagine if crowds of people pressed their noses up against the windows of your home every day. Imagine if they came straight through the front door and started walking through the rooms, opening the drawers and cupboards, checking your visitor's book, and having a good look around. And then, without ever having a conversation with you, they either announced that their house was so much better than yours and skipped away happily, or, with drooping shoulders and a sorrowful expression, murmured, 'Our house is completely inadequate compared to yours.'

Their quick conclusions would seem even stranger if they had seen only half the picture. Maybe they missed several rooms, had no idea about the renovations that were planned, the leaks that appeared in heavy rain, and so much more. It would seem like rather bizarre behaviour, wouldn't it? And yet you are likely to do something similar to yourself when you fall victim to comparison and judgment, and the subsequent expectations that can result.

We live and work in such a hyper-visible and connected online world today that comparing ourselves to others is inevitable. The windows and front door to competitors' businesses are wide open to us through their websites and social-media platforms, and new ones appear all the time. We can find ourselves visiting them too often, obsessing over what services and programs they're offering, how many comments they're getting on their blogs, checking their Facebook and Instagram accounts, seeing how many people are in their groups, evaluating what marketing activities they're implementing, and so on and so on.

Occasionally, these surreptitious forays can be positively affirming as you benchmark yourself. But in my personal experience, and in hearing the stories of dozens of clients, it's far more common that these forays will see you tumbling headfirst into the comparison trap. This can be a pretty demoralising place, teeming with gremlins of doubt that make you feel less than, flattened, confused, and full of uncertainty, sometimes to the point of changing everything you do, or even giving up completely. These gremlins can really get under your skin as they join forces with your inner critic.

You can compare yourself, your business and your achievements with an endless number of people and businesses, and it's all too easy to do so, even when you innocently believe you are just in research mode. That can be a slippery slope because there's always someone who has done something you wish you had achieved or accomplished by now. Most of the time it's an unfair comparison.

How do you know if that incredible program is actually selling? How do you know for sure that the owner of that website is happy and fulfilled with their work? How do you know if the amazingly engaged Facebook group you're lurking in is actually delivering new clients to the founder? How do you know that the pretty average-looking course is not a huge profit producer?

Even if the projected successes you're seeing are true, and you have no real way of knowing for sure, you could be comparing your business beginning with their mature middle, and thus setting even more unrealistic expectations for yourself.

It's equally important to ask yourself if that is the actual business you want. Comparing your unique journey to the equally unique journey of someone else is seldom a helpful business growth strategy.

As well as your own expectations, you also have to recognise the weight of other people's. These can be the most debilitating, especially when they come from people you love and hope will provide you with bottomless support and encouragement. *Are you still playing around with that business idea? Why don't you let it go and get a real job?*

When your results don't reflect your expectations, when people don't respond in the way you feel they should, the ensuing misbeliefs can trigger those feelings of not being enough and erode your sense of worthiness. This downward spiral is not actually set in motion by reality; rather, your thinking triggers it.

The good news is that when you have heightened your self-awareness you can put in place some simple and powerful strategies to mitigate this potentially negative impact.

TRIFECTA, SMART AND HEART GOALS

What happens if you set a goal to have twelve people in your online program and you enrol only seven? Does that define you as a failure? No, of course not. But if your expectation was utterly fixated on achieving that precise number, you can expect your inner critic to pay a gloating visit holding her I-told-you-so sign high.

This is why I encourage all of my clients to set trifecta goals, defining acceptable, stretch and unicorn levels.

For example, for the online program, the acceptable goal may be six participants. This will cover your costs and provide a modest profit margin. The stretch goal might be eight participants. This will easily cover costs and provide a healthy profit margin. The unicorn goal could be set at twelve participants, where you'd be so deliciously excited, you'd literally catch, saddle up and ride a unicorn around the block when you reach it.

The purpose of trifecta goals is twofold. First, they create realistic milestones that encourage you to celebrate your progress rather than hold off until you reach a single, lofty achievement level. And second, they encourage you to loosen your mental grip, to hold your expectations lightly, and gently remind yourself that business ownership does not come with a crystal ball and that you are making progress every single day.

It also helps to pair your head with your heart when it comes to setting goals. You may have heard of SMART, an acronym for goals that are specific, measurable, achievable, realistic, and time-bound. These goals are action oriented and provide focus in a linear way. They certainly have their place in your business, but without balance they can become rigid and demanding. This is why I developed HEART goals to aim for, right alongside SMART goals.

HEART goals are developed to reflect and honour the way you want to feel as you conduct your business. HEART stands for harmonious, engaging, aspirational, refreshing, and transformative. The idea is to blend your goals so they address both sides of the achievement coin, and to ensure that you create an environment that supports the likelihood of achieving these goals. I used a blend of SMART and HEART trifecta goals to write this book, to help to create and manage my own 'expectation environment':

SMART trifecta goal: To write a 35,000-word (acceptable), 40,000-word (stretch) or 50,000-word (unicorn) book that is ready for release by the end of 2020.

HEART trifecta goal: To write a book that provides inspiration and encouragement to women and to enjoy the process by working with an author coach who can encourage, inspire and assist me to write the best book I can.

To support achieving my goals, I also created a working environment that made me feel good whenever I sat down to write, and I recognised and appreciated both my progress as a writer and the progress of the book by rewarding myself as I reached each chapter milestone. There have been a lot of flowers bought, music played, candles lit, aromatherapy oils put in my demister, and fantastic sessions with my author coach as she's coaxed me out of the writing shadows of doubt and into the sunshine of progress.

When we embarked on this writing journey, I was holding on pretty tightly to what I now understand were restrictive expectations about how my own author journey should look and feel. Never having written a book before, these expectations were based purely on fantasy, ideas I had formed largely from watching other people, seemingly magically, whisk a book out of thin air in no time at all.

I was also looking at some of my favourite books from the thousands I've read over the years and thinking that mine needed to be as polished and impactful as those produced by world-famous authors to be of any use. When my thoughts began to work against me, I practised another key skill I've shared with you: catch and detach, I reminded myself, catch and detach.

Interestingly, expectations can be both positive (*I'll manage to write my own book in no time at all*) and negative (*I'll never manage to write anything like what I read, it's going to be agonising*). Like me, you may find yourself in the midst of an interesting quandary or two along the way.

Adopting HEART goals alongside SMART goals is about setting yourself up for success by letting go of externally created beliefs of how things should unfold according to some mythical predetermined schedule. Instead, choose to support yourself in creating the environment and conditions for your own personal flourishing. Start by asking yourself: *What do I need to support me? What would feel good?* And then do that on the schedule that suits you and your life.

DEFINE WHAT SUCCESS MEANS FOR YOU

The curtain has been pulled back, so now what? So far, I've highlighted some of the emotional and thinking traps that can attempt to derail you when you're moving out of the design stage into the delivery stage of your next chapter. If you're feeling a little on edge right now, let me assure you that there's plenty of light at the other end of the tunnel.

The sheer number of solo, micro, small, medium and large businesses out in the world is testament to the inspiration, focus and creativity of an endless number of people committed to self-determination, self-expression and helping others. You, my friend, are definitely one of them.

The actual launch of your business is often a seemingly small event to the world at large as you glide serenely across the water, wee flippers paddling furiously underwater. The door to your café is open. The website is live. The social-media page is up. What now?

First, congratulations are in order. This is a momentous achievement and deserves a significant acknowledgement. I want you to decide what that will look like for you and then celebrate, celebrate, celebrate. You now have one heck of an entry for your fabulous file.

Now the adventure truly begins, as you take your PEP and enact it on a daily and weekly basis. Your experience of delivering your service to the market will depend on the type of business you chose to design, but there are some ideas I'd like to share with you. I know from personal experience and observing my clients that they will likely be helpful for you, too.

With the nature of our online world, you might often find yourself working alone in your home office. But that online world also means you can be connected with a veritable army of kindred spirits right across the globe. The value of having women alongside you who are also walking this path cannot be overestimated, so I encourage you to reach out and connect with others who will be experiencing a similar cocktail of emotions.

Free Facebook groups and paid mastermind programs are where I've met the majority of my online belief buddies. I backed this up by exploring local, in-person networking events and the occasional national conference. Please don't go it alone, the adventure is far more enjoyable when you have company and there are just as many introverts in business as there are extroverted souls. We all crave connection at a soul level.

Some days will feel like they have darted by. You'll find yourself wondering where the time has gone when you've been in flow, mesmerised by your work. On other days you'll feel as though your to-do list is covertly procreating while you're not looking, with tasks that expand to burst the seams of that same period of time.

You'll have days when you despair of ever making progress and will seriously question why you made the decision to go into business at all. You'll also have days when you literally dance around your office in utter delight, ecstatic that this—*this*—is the work you get to do in the world.

All these days will pass and revisit, over and over. It's the nature and fabric of being a businesswoman.

Both you and your business are destined to evolve over time, expanding and changing and refining as you take in feedback and experience mini versions of the Your Next Chapter change cycle dozens of times over. Discontent will visit, letting you know that adjustment is in order again. The one guarantee I can give you is that the business you begin will not be the same business you have in one, three, five, or ten years' time. That is absolutely as it's meant to be as you learn, change and grow. Enjoy the ride.

To help you stay focused on your *why*, especially when you're in the midst of a challenging day, or faced with competing options and need to make decisions, return to your purpose, vision and mission, allowing them to become your anchor, guiding you forward as your training wheels drop off.

I briefly and quietly reflect on mine each morning when I start my day, and a shortened version is at the top of my weekly planner.

Remember that what defines success is deeply personal. I encourage you to take the time to identify what it looks and feels like for you so you can connect with it regularly and ensure you are on the right path for you.

When I asked my community how they measured success, their feedback defied traditional measures.

> *Kirana:* 'By the butterflies in my stomach and the big smile on my face, a feeling of winning.'

> *Lin:* 'When I'm feeling energetic and motivated by the results or outcomes I've created.'

> *Amanda:* 'When I achieve the goals I set out to achieve, large or small, the feeling of warmth usually puts a big smile on my face.'

> *Alison:* 'It's the warm feeling that motivates me to strive for more. Be that helping clients, a tricky yoga pose, a freshly planted tree or a wagging tail as you walk your dog. Success is the feeling from within that tells me I've done a good job, made a difference, that I am enough. It's not based on money, popularity or any other external markers.'

> *Kara:* 'I have a saying that success is a series of incremental upgrades. It's not a destination for me, it's doing better than I've done before.'

> *Pascale:* 'It's that excitement and energy, knowing that I've achieved what I set out to do.'

Tracy: 'The warm feeling inside I get when I realise I've made a positive difference to someone else.'

Kim: 'It's all about freedom of choice, which comes from being financially secure, healthy and mentally well. Success to me is also about seeing my clients rise and be the best version of themselves.'

Donna: 'I think it's a mixture for me. Of course, financial freedom is a great feeling, but more importantly it's the satisfaction of creating something of worth. Sharing our skills and knowledge to bring about change, beauty and growth in others is so fulfilling. So for me success means feeling completely expressed as a person on all levels, that I'm growing and expanding and have found ways of channelling what I have to offer in a magical dance with creation, other people and the world.'

What form does success take for you? How does it look and feel? Take some time to muse and outline your thoughts on how you would like to blend contribution, fulfilment and financial reward for you. What role will each aspect play and how will you recognise it, know that it's taking place?

Focus on adding value and being useful. Your business is a beautiful, powerful expression of you, but it is not you. Your business offerings, products and services represent the value you create and deliver as a result of who you are and how you decide to contribute to the world, and may well vary from year to year. Your own worth is definitive, enduring and unchanging, a completely separate entity that is boundless and ever-present. It's imperative that you don't confuse or fuse the two.

My business may soar, or fold, or hover happily between these two states, but what happens within it is never going to change who I am or my birthright of worthiness.

So with that in mind, be sure to stay connected to the principles of simply being useful to your clients and adding value to their world, rather than trying to prove yourself. Stay clear of the worthiness weeds by being aware that you are simply on a business learning curve, not a quest to gain approval, or gold stars and badges for your blazer. Contribute with a full heart; give from a full cup. You are, without question, already amazing.

You are someone's puzzle piece. They're out there with a wee hole in their world, a gap that only you can help them to close. Don't make them wait any longer. Gather up your courage, your strengths, your insights and lessons and deliver what they've been searching for.

You've got this.

PART FOUR

MAINTAINING MOMENTUM

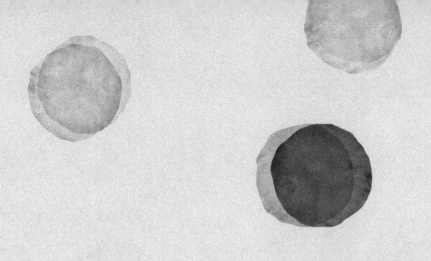

'We're here for a reason and I believe a bit of the reason is to throw little torches out to lead people through the dark.'

Whoopi Goldberg

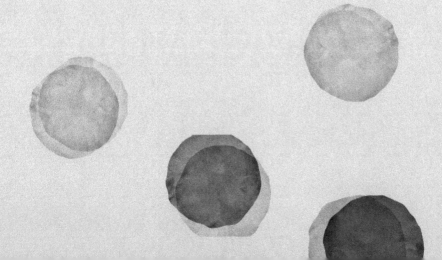

CHAPTER 7

DEDICATION

Continue Your Adventure

'I'm amazed at how quickly I bounce back these days,' Sarah marvelled. 'If you'd hit me with these setbacks even a year ago, I'd be reeling for days. But it's different now. *I'm* different now. I know it's just a blip, and I'm absolutely fine to get up, dust myself off and keep moving.'

This assertion from my client on a recent call had me dancing with delight. The significant changes in presence and self-assurance transforming her business were a direct result of reconnecting to her innate self-worth, which in turn allowed her to genuinely appreciate the value of what she offers to the world. I'd witnessed this gradual change—this deep anchoring to her power and strength—over several years and it was inspiring.

A venture into the world of business is one of the most transformative personal development journeys you'll ever take. You can anticipate a great many challenges as you establish your next-chapter business. And you can also anticipate an incredible trajectory of personal expansion as your confidence, courage and resilience build.

Business demands a lot and it gives a lot in return. Alongside your commitment to mastering the building blocks of business sits your commitment to developing your inner resources.

When you first make the decision to hear what your discontent and desire have to tell you, your inner strength will grow. As you develop your business concept, making more decisions about your brand, the service you offer, how you'll market and sell, your inner strength will grow. When you put your physical or digital shingle up and declare yourself open for business, your inner strength will grow. On the days when customers and clients arrive, and also on the days when they don't arrive, your inner strength will grow again and again and again.

As you work through challenges, figure out solutions, try and fail, try and succeed, pivot, iterate, recalibrate, evolve and learn, you'll be in awe of your capacity—when you allow yourself to. Building a business is seldom easy, but it's frequently fun and often deeply fulfilling. Just like Sarah, there will come a day when you recognise that you've grown to a point where your ability to bounce up has become a part of who you are. And that will be a day to celebrate.

BOUNCING UP

I've seen this phenomenon so often that I've named it the 'bounce-ability' factor. It's not possible to pinpoint its arrival exactly since everyone has their own internal timetable. But if you make the conscious decision to work on developing yourself alongside the decision to work on developing your business, its arrival is inevitable.

It appears to work in a similar way to the principle of compound interest. As you are likely aware, compound interest enriches the value of an original investment; when interest is paid monthly, you earn interest on the sum of the original principle and the interest itself each month. Over time, your principle expands exponentially.

Similarly, you will earn additional interest (extra personal growth) on the typical interest (personal growth) that you earn from your principle investment (your business) each month. And when you make the decision to actively seek that growth, to invest in yourself, it will compound the impact further. You'll reach a point where you suddenly realise you're grounded so strongly in self-awareness, self-compassion and self-belief that your inner core of worthiness is as wide as the sky and as deep as the ocean.

Setbacks, disappointments, things not turning out quite as planned, potential clients choosing not to work with you, launches not bringing in the numbers you hoped—any of these experiences can try to hold you underwater, but they can't define or contain you. They cannot hold you back. The internal force of you is far stronger than any of these minor setbacks, and the vision you have for your business is far more compelling than any obstacle. You'll inevitably break free and surge powerfully to the surface again, bursting through stronger and wiser, adding another experience deposit into your personal self-belief account.

It's a powerful realisation to know that no matter what meets you on the path, you're going to be able to navigate yourself through and stay on track. This is the essence of what you most need for this journey into your next chapter, when you may find yourself assailed by messages of just how many small businesses 'fail' in their quest.

MAKING DEPOSITS INTO YOUR BELIEF BANK

You may have heard these words before, most often delivered in ominous or slightly pitying tones: *You do know that half of all businesses fail in the first year, don't you?* Let's take the scare factor out of this oft-mentioned statement and look calmly at the facts.

In its 2019 report on small business in the Australian economy, the Australian Bureau of Statistics reported that of the 2.25 million businesses operating in 2019, 62.1 percent were sole traders without employees, 27.1 percent were micro businesses (1–4 employees), and 8.5 percent were small businesses (5–19 employees). [21] Together, small businesses contribute 34.2 percent of Australia's gross domestic product. That's a mighty contribution to our families, our communities and our country.

The bureau looked at how many businesses were still operating in June 2019, compared to June 2014. It found that 59.6 percent of solo businesses were still active at this five-year mark, along with 69.3 percent of micro businesses, and 77.6 percent of small businesses. I find that very encouraging, and I hope you do, too.

When pondering this data, it's important to also consider the myriad of reasons that may have prompted business owners to stop or close a business, not all of which are because it wasn't succeeding in the classic revenue-generating sense. Of course, some businesses just don't grow. Some ideas that looked sensational on the drawing board just don't translate successfully into reality, and we need to accept that truth, pause, pivot and move on. However, sometimes the decision to stop is because circumstances have changed, and the owner has chosen to change course.

Sometimes we achieve a goal that was important to us, and we then decide to move on in a different direction. Sometimes the personal development path we're travelling parallel to our business-development experience makes us recognise that change is not only desirable, it's absolutely essential. Often, the choice to close or end something is the very best decision we can make, and becomes the catalyst for a phoenix-like rise into a next chapter that might be a far better fit for us.

But sometimes, sadly, we can lose heart, faith and energy, and that combination makes the decision for us because we don't have external support to rely on to help enhance our bounce-ability.

Fortunately, with self-awareness you can also develop a strong base within yourself. Additional external support then simply provides the finishing touch.

In an earlier chapter we looked at the business clarity fulcrum, the blend of contribution, fulfilment and financial reward that's unique to you and which is at the centre of every next chapter. The starting point is to consciously respond to the pull inside you to address a need you see, and then design a business to deliver your services, solutions and products in a way that feels beautifully aligned with you. You then need to continue to make regular deposits into your belief bank, to work in the fertile space of self-acceptance and self-development so you can focus on what you do on a daily basis and commit to doing it a little better each day.

The greatest investment you can make to ensure the sustainability of your next-chapter business is to maintain a strong connection to your innate self-worth, where your confidence, empathy and resilience (bounce-ability) reside.

This connection ensures that you are open and aware, and responsive to the needs of your clients and the developments in your market. It ensures that you are self-accepting and self-supportive, confident in your current abilities and committed to your continued learning and skill development. It engages your curiosity and creativity, and your ability to dance at your growth edges, open to expansion and new ideas rather than staying safe and seated in your familiar zone.

A healthy connection to self-worth is at the core of every entrepreneur and business owner who recognises the message that discontent delivers, and becomes willing to explore desire instead.

In this final chapter, we'll focus on dedication to the types of actions that will ensure you're able to make regular deposits into your belief bank, strengthening your self-worth connection. I have already covered some of them, making this an important recap, while others will be new.

You can choose to act on the ones that resonate most strongly with you. Personally, I tend to practise them all in micro doses because I've found that each contributes to my growth in a unique way. Woven together, they create a strong, regular self-belief plan.

REVISITING YOUR *WHY*

'Start with your *why*' is guidance that was first offered by author and speaker Simon Sinek in a 2009 TED Talk that has now been watched more than fifty-one million times.[22] He equates an innate sense of purpose with being connected to your personal *why*. According to Sinek, 'People are inspired by a sense of purpose (a *why*) and this should come first when communicating with your audience, even before what, and definitely before how. They don't care what you do, they care why you do it.'

Anchoring your business in a strong sense of what is purposeful and meaningful for you, and standing for something more than simply what you offer and sell, is certainly an effective way of attracting like-minded, aligned clients. It's also one of the most effective ways of connecting you to a bottomless source of focus and energy, giving you the ability to bounce back when you've had a temporary setback because you are on a personal mission.

Some of the questions to contemplate that will help you to deepen your connection to your unique and personal *why*, especially as it evolves over time, include:

- If I had a soapbox to stand on, what beliefs and passions would I talk about?
- Why do I feel this way? Why is it so important?
- What experiences have I had in this area that I can use to create connections with other people?
- How can I show that I understand, that I've been there and that there is a way through?

Checking in with yourself and revisiting these questions regularly will keep you on course. It will ensure you are both inspired and resolute on days when things feel a little tough. It will also allow you to course correct; to make the inevitable small changes as you learn and grow.

When I first launched my mentoring business, I cast a very wide net across the world of women starting and running small businesses, intending to provide my wholehearted blend of support to a broad audience. Over time, however, I recognised that my *why* was changing to align more specifically with my experiences of changing direction in my forties after regaining my sense of worth. My *why* evolved and I responded to that evolution, and that ever-deepening connection contributed to my ability to bounce up, because I was and am, inspired by my vision and my desire to work purposefully.

Your *why* forms the basis of your purpose, vision and mission statement, which we covered in an earlier chapter. I encourage you to write down your *why* and display it where you can see and feel it. I've transposed mine onto a beautiful photo of a lighthouse and my eyes travel to it several times a day. I don't just read the words; I *feel* them.

You can also create a small ritual around your sense of connection when you feel you've lost a little motivation. It can even become a daily practice. Place your hand on your heart. Breathe slowly and deeply. Take a moment to connect to the feelings of contribution and fulfilment, of reaching out, of helping people to flourish and grow and navigate their own challenges, too. Smile. Feel your sense of purpose, determination and joy expand. Now bounce up. You have important work to do in the world.

YOUR SUPPORT CIRCLE

We are not designed to live and work in isolation. A sense of belonging is a basic human need, and the support that flows from feeling connected is as essential as the air we breathe. Strong support becomes even more important when we're stepping outside the realm of potential and into the arena, challenging ourselves. Few things demand personal growth as greedily as being in business for ourselves.

Building a support circle mindfully is a valuable investment in yourself, and I've identified four quadrants within that circle that deserve your attention:

1. *Physical:* Naturally, taking care of your physical needs with good food, hydration and sleep are all important forms of self-support. There have been many times when my enthusiasm and confidence have wavered, and I've realised that it had more to do with a late night and a skipped lunch than a sudden loss of capability.

    But your physical quadrant needs more than just the basics. It encompasses both preventative measures to keep you in good health, and activities you do purely for fun. Mine includes playing soccer, walking, yoga, reflexology and massage, a physiotherapist, and regular visits to the doctor and dentist.

2. *Emotional/spiritual:* By now you've likely recognised the role that emotions play in our business adventures and are committing to adopting some of the practices I've shared with you. An important anchor for me in this quadrant of my support circle includes a conscious connection to a higher power, which I first developed

through the lessons within my 12-step fellowship. We were encouraged to explore our own concept of a higher power, be it God, nature, spirit, the universe or anything else that felt nourishing, reassuring and supportive. We were also encouraged to pursue conscious contact with this power in our own way, on a daily basis.

At first this was quite challenging for me, but I began with a simple connection to nature that came naturally to me after my childhood on our farm. Over time I've gradually learned to lean back into this sensation of feeling supported, that someone or something is there for me, that I'm never alone.

I also have an ongoing relationship with a fabulous counsellor. I talk things through with her when my mind tries to take me into what we've both termed the 'bad neighbourhood' in my brain, where I'm assailed by worries and fears.

Other practices in this quadrant include journaling almost every day and listening to guided meditations to help me connect to a state of inner calm. I end my day with a gratitude list.

I am also immensely grateful for a set of three powerful questions I was taught by a spiritual mentor. I remind myself of them when I'm confronted, triggered or just a little too eager to share my 'infinite wisdom' with someone: Does it need to be said? Does it need to be said by me? Does it need to be said now? These questions can be considered a type of spiritual practice in themselves.

3. *Community:* There is a vast array of communities you can choose to become a part of. You can, of course, also create your own and invite

others to join you. Your communities don't all need to be business focused, but I do recommend having at least one where you're connected with other businesspeople experiencing a similar journey. The sense of camaraderie and understanding with others who 'get it' is important. Their honest feedback and real encouragement will increase your bounce-ability factor immensely.

In this quadrant my recovery community is an ongoing source of strength, keeping me grounded and grateful. I'm both a member and creator of Facebook groups that connect me with women all over the world. I love hosting Next Chapter dinners for women in business, where I introduce personal and business-development topics to discuss over good food. I also go along to networking groups, conferences and events to learn and connect with new people.

4.   *Mindset/mentoring:* One of my highest values is learning. I'm always on a quest to expand what I know and to share my lessons with others, and that applies particularly to working on my mindset, expanding what I see as possible for me. Today the foundation of this is books, books, books and more books. I have a small library in my home, and I read widely and deeply.

I've also learned to appreciate the value of investing in mentorship and coaching. When I was running my marketing agency, I held the misbelief that I needed to know it all, that asking for help would somehow weaken my position as a consultant. That narrow thinking kept me stuck for longer than I care to recall. Now I invest in programs, experiences and people that help me to close specific skill gaps, and I'm seldom without the support of a mastermind or personal mentor to help me continue to live and work at my growth edge.

Take some time to consider your own support circle and see if there are gaps in these quadrants that you can gradually fill. The best place to start is to secure a belief buddy, someone you can share your vision with who understands why it's important to you and commits to being there to support you on both good and bad days. You can become that same anchor for them as well.

I treasure each of my belief buddies. They have kept me afloat through some incredibly tough times and have often played the main roles in each of my support quadrants. I hope I've done the same for them.

THE BOOKENDS OF YOUR DAY

This is a simple practice that builds a foundation of daily calm and focus. It's especially helpful if you're prone, as I am, to popcorn brain: a mind that is constantly on the go, peppering you with ideas and priorities from the moment you wake up until you're ready for rest at night. Creating a nourishing routine helps you to mindfully ease into and out of each day. It provides you with two distinct windows of opportunity to value yourself and enhance and support your self-worth connection before you begin to work with and for anyone else. And this includes your family.

Ask yourself how you start and end each day at the moment. Could you benefit from defining a space for you? What could you introduce that could anchor you more intentionally?

My morning bookends:

- A short visualisation or guided meditation
- Journaling while enjoying a cup of tea
- Selecting an essential oil for the diffuser in my office
- Playing particular music to get me started

My evening bookends:

- Turning off my computer and not just allowing it to go into sleep mode; with a home office I've found it too tempting to do *just one more thing* when I leave the computer on
- Switching off from social media at least an hour before bed
- Reading an inspiring piece of writing
- Writing a gratitude list

What will you adopt as your bookends? You may also like to adopt the extra step of identifying the 'park benches' of your day, specific times when you will consciously pause and re-energise yourself by moving away from your desk, stepping outdoors, playing a piece of music, practising box breathing, or striking a yoga pose or two.

SKYLIGHT THINKING

A key skill to develop as you move forward in your next chapter is your ability to adopt a positive permission/decision flow when you're faced with a challenge. It can be easy to fall into what I call the 'problem trap', especially when you're on a learning curve and in the early stages of business building, when you're still developing your voice and vision. I've spent enough time floundering around in problem thinking to recognise its characteristics and pitfalls, and I created an alternative approach that is far more effective.

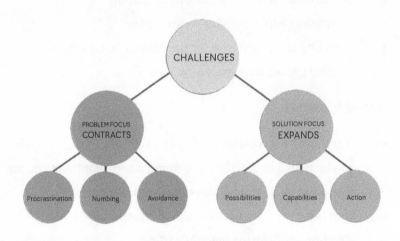

Skylight Thinking

You know you're stuck in the problem trap when you feel blocked and flat. Your body feels contracted, and you can almost feel yourself taking up less space as you turn inwards. Fresh ideas are in short supply and you begin the negative thought spiral that often starts with the suspicion that you're not up to the task in front of you, or that success is for other people.

This draining of your creativity and positivity occurs because what you focus on grows. Negative thoughts begin to gain momentum, crowding out your bounce-up thoughts and creativity, and you begin to shut down or feel overwhelmed.

When you focus on the problem, your thoughts are dominated by the multitude of reasons why you cannot or will not be able to create or achieve what you want. Your brain fixates on the impossibility until you're in danger of becoming a victim of the circumstance.

Problem-trap thoughts:

- My problem is that not enough people know about me.
- My problem is that my audience or list is too small.
- My problem is that I suck at sales conversations.
- My problem is that there are already too many people who do what I do.

Can you hear the inner-critic overtones in that thinking? By now you know that your inner critic is often waiting in the wings, eager for an invitation, even an unconscious one, to step into the limelight and throw her weight around.

When you begin to feel overwhelmed and deflated, believing that what you want is out of your reach or capabilities, your next most likely step is into the escape hatch. *This is an uncomfortable feeling. I don't want to experience that. I'll just …*

And then you dive into your own version of liberation. It could be spending time on Facebook, fiddling with admin, diving headfirst into deep research mode in the search for another course or program to close your perceived gaps, eating chocolate, switching on Netflix, or whatever numbing behaviour or distraction appeals to you.

In my masterminds we often laugh as we identify our 'productive procrastination' techniques, recognising that no matter how apparently important our suddenly urgent alternative activities may appear to be on the surface, they're usually a mirage.

I'm all for taking time out and revitalising yourself if you're simply a little brain dead and need to withdraw for a while to allow inspiration to resurface. The trick is to differentiate between this positive self-care strategy and pure avoidance behaviours and habits.

If you do recognise a tendency to tip into avoidance or problem-trap thinking, you can choose to quickly flip your thinking into the solution-focus realm instead.

When you consciously focus on a solution you choose to concentrate on the desired outcome and the feeling of accomplishment and progress you're looking for. This allows you to use your amazingly creative brain to open a skylight instead of a trap, to find the answers, options and ideas you need. Your brain is primed to answer questions, so ask it to focus in a more positive and expansive way.

To open the skylight with inspired thoughts and emotions, ask yourself:

- What do I want to create?
- Where's the opportunity?
- What's right about this?
- Why is it so easy for me to find a way through?
- What's the fabulous outcome I'm going to create?
- How will I feel when this happens?
- Who will it help?

As you change your focus, you will feel your emotions begin to move and bounce up, and will quickly begin to brainstorm ideas and action steps you can take to get you started and overcome inertia. Remember, actions of confidence come before feelings of confidence. When you're in motion, your brain tends to get unstuck and your confidence begins to remember that its purpose in life is to help you.

You can make the conscious decision to move from the contracted-problem trap to a creative-solution focus. You can open a skylight into a new possibility, break through the inertia and begin to create and build again.

THE POWER OF THE PAUSE

Moving through business and life strongly connected to your self-awareness is an unquestionable advantage. When you're committed to being aware of what's going on inside your body and your mind, you can pause and practise discernment. When something triggers you, you can exercise your ability to respond consciously and thoughtfully to challenges rather than react emotionally.

For me, it always starts in the body. If something or someone triggers me, I feel myself tense and clench and then, invariably, my body heats up. The adrenaline surge hits, and I find myself pulling inwards, ready to attack, defend or shut down. None of those states, as you can imagine, are conducive to progress and making good decisions. Now when I feel the tension arrive, I recognise it. Rather than the trigger to react, it's become a trigger to pause, anchor myself and allow space to dissipate the charge associated with the trigger.

Some of my favourite anchoring exercises:

- *Box breathing*, a slow, deep, quiet breathing technique: To practise this calming method, breathe in for a count of four, hold for a count of four, breathe out for a count of four, pause for a count of four, and start the process again.

I've found that four or five rounds of box breathing slow me down sufficiently to have the smart part of my brain, the cerebral cortex, come back online. Then I can confidently take the reins from the reactionary, energetic parts that are ready to fight but are not particularly reliable or sensible.

- *Heightened-awareness listening:* Pause, close your eyes and listen intently for the sounds that are farthest away. Just listen and note them for a few moments, then switch your attention to the sounds closest to you. Alternating between these two states for just three to four minutes invariably settles and anchors me in the present space again, with access to my full power.

- *Touch awareness:* Close your eyes and rub your thumb back and forth across the first two fingers of your right hand, performing the motion slowly and deliberately, paying acute attention to the subtle sensations this evokes. This exercise slows you down, helping you become calm and present again. Your breathing usually slows at the same time, adding to the sense of peace.

- *Visual awareness:* Allow your eyes to rest on a specific object or scene in your surroundings. Slowly, carefully, with a spirit of appreciation, allow your eyes to travel over it and see it in new ways. Note each curve and line, and colour and texture. The unhurried nature of your visual exploration gently assuages the tension, focuses your mind and allows you to reach that space of calm awareness again.

For a long time, I had a significant charge around not having a university degree. My youthful foray into higher education in New Zealand was short-lived, interrupted by a holiday in Sydney that has so far lasted more than thirty years. I have felt distinctly not good enough because of this perceived deficiency, and I've invested much time and thought into addressing the misbelief, pausing and focusing on dissipating the often-debilitating sense of lack.

I've come to understand the key reasons I felt this way. In New Zealand in the eighties, only around fifteen percent of high school students went on to university, and I saw those individuals as belonging to a special, elevated club that I wanted to be a member of. Additionally, my parents quietly hoped that I'd be the first of my immediate family to manage this achievement, intensifying the pressure I placed on myself. I fused with a deep sense of inadequacy when I didn't achieve this goal, coming to Australia and starting work instead.

This misbelief about my limited capabilities because of my lack of degree qualifications (even though I subsequently gained a marketing diploma at technical college by attending three years of evening lectures), has been a large part of why I've hesitated to put my thoughts into a book. Negative thinking restrained my actions for so long: *Who am I to think I'll be able to write anything good enough? After all, I'm not even qualified.*

But then something happened that made me realise that this misbelief had finally shifted.

I was talking with a colleague about my need for assistance with an upcoming market-research project. The conversation turned to who might be able to help me in the field of academia, leading to questions relating to my own background. She expressed surprise that I had not completed university. This observation, even though it was entirely devoid of judgment, would have been a ferocious trigger for me in the past. The lovely Helga would have stepped forward, delighting in the opportunity to make me squirm.

But this time, as I checked in with myself, anticipating the tense-and-clench reaction that historically has always accompanied such a moment, I discovered there was nothing there. There was absolutely no charge.

What a momentous, delightful, magnificent experience that was! In the past, my reaction would have affected the entire conversation, hijacking my thoughts, causing me to react defensively, and sending me down thought tunnels of inadequacy. I would have missed the opportunity for the learning, help and growth that was on offer.

I revelled in how clear and free I was, being able to distinguish between who I am, and what I have done or not done. I realised with a joy jolt that a deep connection to unconditional, consistent self-worth rather than an achievement-oriented, conditional and fleeting sense of self-esteem was setting me free in more ways than I could have imagined.

The release from such a significant misbelief about not being enough was a classic fabulous-file moment that had nothing to do with gathering and storing feedback or testimonials.

Tangible proof of your ability is a core component of your fabulous file, your confidence-boosting dossier, but that's not all it can contain. Also recognise and honour the significance of moments where you've had your own powerful breakthroughs. Don't just brush them aside. They're too important for casual dismissal.

I wrote a note to myself celebrating the disappearance of the charge, which was replaced by calm acceptance and the knowledge that I am enough exactly as I am today. At some point in the future I may choose to return to university and study, but that choice will no longer be determined by a sense of neediness and lack. I will make my decision from a place of worth, curiosity and personal fulfilment. That's what I want for you, too. Make your choices from a joyful desire for expansion, rather than a need to prove a single thing to anyone.

WHAT WILL UNFOLD IN YOUR NEXT CHAPTER?

Since 2006, when I was first immersed in the world of acceptance, love, forgiveness and beauty, the wild freedom of possibility that the recovery movement represents for me, I have often stood at the front of a room full of fellow travellers and retold my story.

We are encouraged to share our experience, strength and hope openly so that others are given the opportunity to identify with the snippets of our stories that reflect their own experiences. We're also encouraged to listen for the similarities, not the differences. I like to think I've opened a skylight for others during the dozens of times I've shared my story, in the same way that a skylight has so often been held open for me.

When you're early in recovery, it's almost impossible to believe that the kind of future the other speakers share is available to you. It seems so far away. So utterly different from the reality you're in at the time, which is filled with fear and uncertainty, doubt and shame. But when you listen to the stories, when you begin to rise just slightly above your own current circumstances and really hear them and the promises they hold, rather than staying closed and scared, something begins to happen.

You begin to feel hope.

That's all you need to begin your own journey. Just that small seed of hope that you can tentatively choose to nourish and nurture, so it has the opportunity to grow into something beautiful.

The first night that I felt that ember of hope awaken inside of me I couldn't possibly have imagined the transformation waiting for me. I was sitting at the back of the room, trying very hard to make myself as invisible as possible. I felt a deadening mixture of resentment, fear and desolation. I was in rehab. In *rehab*. This was not a milestone I ever expected to be marking. My kids were at home without me. It was my wedding anniversary. My fledgling business was in limbo. I was cocooned in shame, not able to see past this confronting reality.

But gradually the story the speaker was sharing began to filter through the protective layers I'd woven around me. She spoke of having been where I was right now. Of how afraid she had been. She shared what it had been like, what happened, and what her life was like now.

She was eloquent. Honest, completely open, and full of hope and joy and confidence. She admitted to bumps on the road, even laughed about them with gentle self-deprecation. She spoke of how much she had learned and grown, of progress, not perfection. And she encouraged us to look back gently and acknowledge where we were, to take stock of our sadness and pain, and then to take complete responsibility for our situation and fully commit to our expansive future.

She was the catalyst I needed.

Two years later, I found myself back at the same rehabilitation centre. This time, I was the guest. This time, I shared my story and encouraged the men and women who were beginning their own journeys to reconnect to their worth, to believe in themselves, to know they were fully capable of writing a new story and beginning their next chapter, too.

* * *

Remember, there are three steps in this journey to a deep connection to self-worth.

First, you believe in me. I'm not able to see my own potential, my own uniqueness, the possibilities available to me. You're able to see further than I can today.

Second, I begin to believe in you and what you see as possible for me. I recognise the value of your experience even if I can't quite yet appreciate my own. I begin to open up. I begin to feel something different might be possible.

Third, eventually, in time, I believe in me and the door swings open to a whole new world.

Some fourteen years later, I have dozens of mini chapters behind me and every single one is shaping me, helping me to become the woman I was always meant to be. Every experience is enriching my ability to contribute to the world. Every experience, no matter how vexing, challenging or even downright frustrating, eventually adds to my sense of fulfilment, adding exponential value to my belief bank.

I've never had to be on this journey alone. I've been beautifully seen, heard, understood and supported by individuals and communities. I've also had the opportunity to give back, sharing my own lessons and helping others to see their own value and potential.

I wish I could fast forward you into your future. I trust I'm contributing to your understanding that you are magnificent, unique; that you are the sky. The desire to create and contribute what's within you is there for a simple, powerful reason. We are all here to help others. That's what life is about. We're all big, beautiful, messy, magnificent mosaics without boundaries or paradigms, and we all have an exceptional ability to make a difference in this world when we commit to ourselves and focus on others.

Please don't wait until you have all of your ducks in a row. Perfectionism in terms of the levels of experience of expertise you feel you need, of how your brand needs to look, of how well developed your website needs to be, of how confident you need to feel—these misbeliefs are the tools of your inner critic.

You need to be only a few steps ahead of the people you're here to serve to be able to help them. I've asked myself often where I might be if the woman who inspired my recovery journey all those years ago had decided she wasn't ready to share her story, hadn't yet made enough progress, or wasn't good enough to be of service.

I want you to pause and visualise someone in the world who is in need. Someone you know you can help. Someone who, when they discover your message, your story, your service, your solution, will catch their breath and feel that hit in their heart, the sudden arrival of hope. They're ignited. And their life is going to be different as a result. That's the power of you.

Your next chapter is calling. How will you respond?

ABOUT THE AUTHOR

ANGELA RASPASS

Angela Raspass is a speaker, podcaster, self-worth advocate, and a mentor for women who are yearning to step into their Next Chapter – their full potential, in business and life. She brings a valuable and appealing combination of insight, empathy and experience to her programs, retreats, speaking engagements and the guest interviews on her podcast.

In 2003, after a corporate career in marketing, events and sponsorships, she launched a marketing agency from her dining room table and grew it to the point where she bought an office on the northside of Sydney and had a small full-time team.

By 2012 Angela realised she had created a business that leveraged her skills and experience but no longer fully engaged her heart. It wasn't a fit for who she had become, a woman utterly changed by overcoming addiction, reconnecting with her self-worth, and developing a fresh vision and mission.

Once you've written a new story of being enough, once you know your value, once you change from the inside out, it can never be business-as-usual again.

After closing her agency and pivoting from consulting to mentoring, Angela now shares a potent blend of personal and business development tools that help her clients uncover, live and work by what's true for them too, building businesses and lives that blend contribution, fulfilment and financial reward.

Angela is also the founder of the Self-Worth Institute, where she offers a Facilitators' Certification Program for leaders, coaches, trainers, wellness advocates, and other professionals. The tools and practices she teaches will reconnect and anchor your clients, colleagues, teams, and communities in self-worth, ensuring your own programs and services are then able to be more fully absorbed and actioned.

Angela is a book lover, a journal collector, a soccer player and a life-long learner. She lives in Bayview, on Sydney's Northern Beaches, with her husband and daughter. Their son is studying at ANU in Canberra.

YOU ARE INVITED TO ACCESS THE MANY RESOURCES AVAILABLE TO INSPIRE AND SUPPORT YOU IN BRINGING THE IDEAS IN THIS BOOK TO LIFE THROUGH ANGELA'S WEBSITE AT WWW.ANGELARASPASS.COM.

YOUR JOURNEY BOARD

- A FREE ONLINE PROGRAM -

Angela's free program, Your Journey Board, is the perfect starting point to help you to develop a purpose and vision statement for Your Next Chapter. The program includes audio guides and downloadable PDF workbooks across three modules:

Module One: Finding the Gold in Your Past
Module Two: Connecting to Your Present Power
Module Three: Developing a Clear Vision for Your Next Chapter

You can access this and other bonus materials at
www.angelaraspass.com/bookbonuses.

A FINAL NOTE FROM ANGELA

If you have enjoyed this book, I'd be grateful if you could take a few minutes to leave an Amazon review or share this link –
www.angelaraspass.com/yournextchapterbook.

Your encouraging words may just inspire another woman to read
Your Next Chapter and change her life as well.

ACKNOWLEDGEMENTS

The people who know me well know of my all-encompassing love for books. I've often joked that the money I've invested in them over the years could easily have bought me a small house. So, you might imagine that writing one myself would be a pretty easy task, since I've been exposed to so many great examples. Not so. Turning my burning, almost life-long desire to write my own book into reality felt a whole lot harder because I *had* seen so many brilliant books, and without support it may never have happened. The experience has been both challenging and rewarding, and I want to thank the fabulous people who have helped make this happen.

Firstly, to Graham, Cameron and Charlotte, thank you for cheering me along every step of the way, for listening to my fears, celebrating my progress, making the space for me to disappear into the world of words, and simply believing in me, completely. I love you all enormously.

To my dear friend Sarah, who gifted me with wholehearted encouragement at every step and was my compassionate first reader, it is an absolute a joy to have you in my life. Thank you for your beautiful, vulnerable, courageous self.

To my dearest Carolyn, the first person outside of my family to whom I confessed my desire to write a book, your absolute conviction that I could was my catalyst to start, and your unwavering belief in my ability was a constant touchstone throughout the journey. Thank you for your inspiration.

To Sonja, who helped me pull all of the ideas out of my head and onto paper, I suspect they may never have seen the light of day without your help and generous insights into your own writing journey. I am so grateful.

To Larissa, who helped me to quiet my doubt and make space for my creativity, I so appreciate our sessions, which always expand my thinking.

To Michelle, who introduced me to the genius mind writing process that helped the words flow, and helped me to understand the value of uncompromising certainty and to recognise and stand in my truth, I am bolder and more deeply connected to my worth because of you. My deepest thanks.

And to Sam, Jo and Donna, who were gentle and generous early readers, your support means the world to me. Thank you.

To Candice, the most fabulous author coach a person could ask for, thank you for striking the perfect balance as you challenged me, stretched me, soothed me and guided me. No matter what I was thinking or feeling, good, bad or in between, you were just always there to listen and then thoughtfully share your insights and wisdom, delivered with your uniquely inspiring blend of calm and humour. I'll be back to write the next one.

To Bev, who I trusted with my wee book baby, to take her from a Google doc and turn her into a real, live in-my-hands book, thank you for being such a smooth operator; your expertise, ideas and connections made the whole daunting process so much easier.

To my friends and supporters in the book-buddy group, thank you for being so generous with sharing your experiences, thoughts and feedback. It's a better book with the richness of your contributions: Mags, Jo, Anita, Sharleen, Janet, Patricia, Kirana, Shan, Sal, Nancy, Kim, Lynne, Diana, Kylie, Lisa, Alison, Jane, Tracey, Joanne, Donna, Jo, Amanda, Jodi, Lian, Sarah, Tracy, Pascale, Shelley and Kara. Thank you.

A sincere thank-you to the way-showers who have inspired me: Brené Brown, Barbara Huson and Kristin Neff.

And finally, my profound gratitude for the Recovery Movement that saved my life.

YOUR NEXT CHAPTER MANIFESTO

What I Believe

SELF-BELIEF is your Super Power

NEXT CHAPTERS are built on *skinned knees* where BREAKDOWNS become BREAKTHROUGHS...

Allow yourself to be fully *seen* and put good things into the world. It's through YOUR STORY that others will find their path, and what a *joy* and a privilege that is.

Everything you need is inside of you now. *Search for it.*
Give yourself PERMISSION to shine.

Life is too short not to be doing the work in the world you're here for.

Your WORTH is *unquestionable*

Stay connected to your truth and always speak to yourself with compassion and encouragement.

Cultivate a circle of support. Surround yourself with people who are real and connect with them deeply through experience. Share with genuine vulnerability.

Your business needs to serve you just as much as you serve your clients. Sustaining your energy and enthusiasm is the goal.

There is no 'perfect'. There is no magic formula. There's only the right way for you, which you'll find through experience, failures and kindsight.

Create your own definition of success. Make meaning your mission, contribution your focus and fulfilment your reward. Know that profit is the result of the right action.

Respond. Don't react.

Find the power of the pause and allow yourself time to grow. This is an EVOLUTION, not a REVOLUTION.

Remember that growth doesn't always mean bigger. It can *mean deeper*

Step up and launch the ideas swirling in your HEAD and your HEART.
Serve the people who need this now.
They're waiting...

YOU'VE *Got this!*
www.angelaraspass.com

YOUR VALUES

Values are an inherent part of you, developed over time and shaped by your internal drives, external experiences and observations. They just are, and don't require explanation or justification, but you'll benefit from being aware of them and choosing to wrap your business core around them. I recommend working with around six core values and being aware of what they look like in action.

This list is intended as a prompt for you. It's not exhaustive, and if your value is missing from the list that doesn't mean it's not valid. To help you narrow down your list, look at grouping together words with a similar meaning. For example, although *achievement* and *accomplishment* have a similar meaning one will probably be a better fit for you. Have fun with this.

Accomplishment	Focus	Partnership
Accuracy	Freedom	Peace
Achievement	Friendships	Personal power
Acknowledgement	Full self-expression	Pleasure
Action	Fun	Poise
Adventure	Generosity	Popularity
Authenticity	Growth	Positivity
Authority	Happiness	Productivity
Autonomy	Harmony	Recognition
Balance	Health/wellbeing	Religion
Beauty	Honesty	Reputation
Boldness	Humour	Resilience
Certainty	Independence	Resolve
Challenge	Influence	Respect
Citizenship	Inner harmony	Responsibility
Clarity	Innovation	Risk taking
Collaboration	Integrity	Romance
Community	Intelligence	Security
Compassion	Intimacy	Self-reliance
Competency	Joy	Self-respect
Connection	Justice	Service
Contribution	Kindness	Spirituality
Creativity	Knowledge	Stability
Curiosity	Lack of pretence	Status
Determination	Leadership	Success
Directness	Learning	Technology
Elegance	Love	To be known
Empowerment	Loyalty	Tradition
Excellence	Mastery	Tranquillity
Fairness	Meaningful work	Trustworthiness
Faith	Nurturing	Wealth
Fame	Openness	Wisdom
Financial abundance	Optimism	Vitality
Flexibility	Orderliness	Zest

REFERENCES

1   https://www.asbfeo.gov.au/sites/default/files/documents/ ASBFEO-small-business-counts2019.pdf

2   https://www.sciencedaily.com/releases/2019/12/191210131935. htm

3   https://www.washingtonpost.com/opinions/2020/01/09/ gen-x-women-middle-age-is-exhausting-heres-why/

4   https://www.instyle.com/celebrity/brene-brown-badass-women

5   https://thework.com/wp-content/uploads/2019/02/Emotions_ List_Ltr.pdf

6   http://www.laughteronlineuniversity.com/ practice-hooponopono-four-simple-steps/

7   https://www.franklincovey.com/the-7-habits/habit-2.html

8   https://www.instinctivedrives.com/

9   Sandberg, Sheryl, 2013. *Lean in: Women, Work and the Will to Lead*, WH Allen

10 https://www.theatlantic.com/magazine/archive/2014/05/ the-confidence-gap/359815/

11 http://www.susanjeffers.com/home/5truths.cfm

12   http://www.danielgoleman.info/topics/emotional-intelligence/

13   (https://positivepsychology.com/act-acceptance-and-com-
      mitment-therapy/#:~:text=Hayes percent20and percen-
      t20ACT-,Steven percent20C.,avoided percent20and
      percent20buffered percent20whenever percent20possible.

14   https://www.drwaynedyer.com/blog/making-the-shift/

15   https://en.wikipedia.org/wiki/Rumi

16   https://medium.com/age-of-awareness/the-4-questions-
      you-must-ask-before-any-decision-cartesian-coordinates-
      47198d2f0809

17   https://www.gallup.com/cliftonstrengths/en/253850/clifton-
      strengths-for-individuals.aspx

18   https://carolyntate.co/

19   https://www.apa.org/pubs/journals/releases/xge-a0035325.pdf

20   https://www.gottman.com/blog/
      the-magic-relationship-ratio-according-science/

21   https://www.asbfeo.gov.au/sites/default/files/documents/
      ASBFEO-small-business-counts2019.pdf

22   https://www.ted.com/talks/
      simon_sinek_how_great_leaders_inspire_action?language=en